SCANDINAVIAN COOKING

Beryl Frank

WEATHERVANE
BOOKS

contents

introduction to scandinavian cooking

This cookbook does not offer exotic dishes such as roast reindeer — who can find a 6- to 8-pound leg of deer in the local supermarket? Hopefully, this book is an excursion to some new taste treats from Scandinavian countries — treats that can easily be made a part of the American cuisine.

Scandinavia — the land of the Midnight Sun — is in northern Europe and includes Sweden, Norway, Denmark, Finland, and Iceland. These five countries share much in common besides their long summer days and long winter nights. They all are water-bound lands that depend on the bounty of the oceans, seas, lakes, and fjords. They breed hardy people who work their fields and forests as well as the sea. They also produce excellent cooks who know how to satisfy family appetites and extend gracious hospitality to guests who come to their homes.

For generations prior to the twentieth century the people of Scandinavia were shut off from the outside world. The sea was their link with other civilizations. Often the water was even the way for a family to go to church, a boat being the only means of travel in the snow-covered land. Cold, hard winters also served to isolate Scandinavians.

Having comparable climatic conditions created similarities among the Scandinavian peoples. These can be seen in their cooking. Herring, which was and is used in all five countries, is often prepared in a like manner in each country. The herring balls made in Sweden may also be made in any or all the other countries. This is true of many of the recipes in this book. The country of origin for a particular food is not necessarily the only country that prepares that food. It is because of these similarities, as well as the differences, that this is called Scandinavian cookery and not Swedish, Norwegian, Danish, Finnish, or Icelandic cookery.

the recipes

If you are a novice cook, follow the recipes exactly. Instructions are, hopefully, complete and accurate. If you have been cooking for a long time, however, and usually do your deep-frying in a 10-inch skillet, do your own thing.

To be safe, most recipes call for the use of a greased pan. (The natural vegetable sprays work very well.) There are some recipes, though, that may not need this. If your pan is seasoned well and you never grease it to make cookies, you will know you do not have to grease the pan.

For the bread recipes it is the cook's option whether to use compressed yeast or active dry yeast. They are interchangeable.

Although butter is generously used in most Scandinavian recipes, it is nearly always possible to substitute margarine for butter. For those who cannot use cream (such as people on cholesterol-free diets), many of the recipes will work well with skim milk.

All the recipes included here were chosen with two ideas in mind: using foods that can be found here in our own markets or in our own homes, and also using foods that were tasty and have the flavor of the Scandinavian countries.

However, you should find new taste treats. For instance, invest in a new spice — cardamom for instance. A little goes a long way, and you will have added a new flavor to your cooking. Try one of the fruit soups — delicious concoctions that will please young and old alike.

Be sure you have an old-fashioned wooden spoon around. While some of the recipes included here can be worked with an electric beater, many are best done by hand — and there is a good feel to stirring with a wooden spoon.

Above all, as you browse through this cookbook, think of the homemakers who live in far-off Scandinavian countries. They are like you — wanting to make mealtimes pleasant with attractively served foods to tempt hearty appetites.

No cookbook is ever complete. One culinary experience invariably leads to another. The recipes included here all share the Scandinavian flavor. Most can be made with ingredients usually found in the home or at a local market.

Whether you are a novice cook, an average family homemaker, or a dedicated gourmet, the cooking of Scandinavia offers happy additions to any menu. Hopefully, you will find many such additions to your menus here.

the smorgasbord

Often the first thought that comes to mind for a traveler through the Scandinavian countries is the traditional smorgasbord. No one can see the tables laden with herring, salmon, caviar, varieties of bread, and thin-sliced meats and not carry the taste-bud memories for the rest of his life.

The word *smorgasbord* means bread-and-butter table. Needless to say, there is more than just bread and butter on the table. It is a tastefully arranged buffet of many different foods — so many as to challenge and defeat even the heartiest of appetites. What a delightful way to be defeated, though, for just as the eater is more than satisfied, a fresh, clean plate is brought to him and there are still more delicacies to try.

The original smorgasbord may date back to Viking feasts. It is known that the Vikings considered hospitality to be more than a virtue — it was a way of life. The visitor had to be fed well. The Viking feasts of long ago brought many guests, and all were welcome. Guests came from great distances and did not come empty-handed. Gifts of food were a common occurrence at the feast and added to the number and kinds of food shared by all.

Was there one huge center table at the Viking feasts, onto which all the food was arranged? Was the food stacked on slices from the large loaves of bread to provide plates for the unknown number of guests? Was the food primarily cold? Was it of the light variety that tempts an appetite prior to a big meal? Were main dishes included? Were there desserts?

To judge by the traditions that have reached the twentieth century, the answer to all these questions can be yes. Common to all smorgasbords, whichever Scandinavian country you are in, is the center table on which all the food is attractively displayed for your gourmet pleasure. Of course, it does not matter whether or not the buffet is in the center of the room — the table will be heavy with delicious food.

The open-faced sandwiches so prevalent in Denmark may have their origin from the Viking feasts. They may be a modern evolution from a long time ago when rounds of bread were used instead of plates. They are eaten today with a knife and fork and offer a limitless variety of simple and elaborate fare. A sandwich may be as simple as thin apple slices with jelly on a thin slice of buttered bread — or as elaborate as smoked salmon on white bread with scrambled eggs on top, served hot. The variety is endless and depends on the creativity of the cook.

The smorgasbord can be a group of appetizers offered prior to a large meal. Anchovy sticks, liver loaf, and Swedish meatballs, to say nothing of the many combinations of herring and other delicacies from the sea, all have their place on such a table. If you indulge too heavily in this type of smorgasbord, however, you may not want anything after it. Scandinavian appetizers are filling.

Hot main dishes can be included on a smorgasbord. Pastry-covered meat loaf, beef roll, and ham rolls are always popular. The array of hot and cold vegetables, fruits, and salads can be as elaborate as you want to make it.

One delightful lagniappe from the smorgasbord is that there are usually marvelous leftovers for the family to eat later. This is a good inducement to add one or two extra platters. The food is so good it will never go to waste.

For those who still have room, there is always the dessert plate. Here everything can be arranged — from fresh fruit with brandy sauce to Tiger Cake or Christmas Cookies. In common with the rest of the smorgasbord, the problem will be what to choose.

The only thing missing from this smorgasbord is the liquid refreshment of Scandinavia. Coffee is always popular. But the Scandinavian palate enjoys beer, ale, and aquavit as well. The climax of the smorgasbord could very well be a light fruit cordial.

There is no meal more memorable for both host and guests than the Scandinavian smorgasbord. Many of the recipes included here adapt well to the buffet table. Plan your next party in the Scandinavian style. It is sure to be fun and good eating for one and all.

appetizers

swedish meatballs
sweden

This recipe improves if made one day ahead of time.

1 pound ground beef
¼ pound ground veal
¼ pound ground pork
2 cups bread crumbs
½ cup milk
1 onion
2 tablespoons butter
2½ teaspoons salt
¼ teaspoon pepper
2 teaspoons nutmeg
2 teaspoons paprika
1 teaspoon dry mustard

3 beaten eggs
¼ cup butter

sauce
Fat left in skillet
¼ teaspoon garlic
5 tablespoons butter
2 teaspoons tomato paste
1 teaspoon beef concentrate
2 cups bouillon or beef stock
1 teaspoon aromatic bitters
 (optional)

Have all the meats ground together twice.

Soak the bread crumbs in milk. Add the meat, and mix together.

Sauté the onion in about 2 tablespoons of butter. Mix the rest of the ingredients, except the ¼ cup of butter, with the onion; put all together with the meat. Mix well and form into 48 small balls. Brown the meatballs in ¼ cup butter. Remove the meatballs and set them aside.

To make the sauce, add the garlic and 1 tablespoon of the butter to the fat left in the skillet. Blend in the rest of the butter and the remaining ingredients. Stir this mixture over low heat until it thickens. Then pour the sauce into a casserole. Stir in 1 cup of sour cream.

Last, add the meatballs to the sauce. Heat the casserole in a moderate oven until it is hot. Makes 48 balls.

liver
loaf
denmark

1 pound calf or chicken livers
1 medium onion
¼ cup butter
¼ cup flour
½ cup heavy cream
½ cup chicken broth

¼ pound pork or beef fat,
    chopped
2 eggs
1 teaspoon salt
½ teaspoon pepper
5 anchovies or 2 tablespoons
    anchovy paste

Put the raw liver and onion through a food chopper.

In a large skillet melt the butter and blend in the flour. Pour in the cream and broth slowly while stirring, then add the chopped fat. When this mixture is thickened and smooth, add the rest of the ingredients. Blend all together thoroughly.

Grease a baking dish or loaf pan and pour the mixture into the prepared dish. Set this in a pan of hot water and bake it in a 350°F oven for 1 hour or more. If needed, add more water to the hot-water bath. The liver is done when a testing knife comes out clean.

Chill the loaf and serve it as is, or slice it for smorgasbord sandwiches. Makes 8 servings.

anchovy
sandwiches
sweden

½ loaf day-old
    homemade-type bread,
    unsliced
10 anchovy fillets
4 tablespoons softened butter
2 tablespoons prepared
    mustard
4 hard-cooked eggs, finely
    chopped

¼ cup chopped dill or ¼ cup
    dill, parsley, and chives
    combined
Dash of freshly ground black
    pepper
Vegetable oil combined with
    butter for frying (about 2
    tablespoons of each)

Trim the crusts from the bread and slice it into 12 thin slices about ⅛ inch thick.

In a small bowl chop the anchovies and mash them together with the butter, mustard, finely chopped eggs, herbs, and pepper. Spread this smooth mixture on 6 slices of the bread. Top each slice with its covering piece of bread. Refrigerate them for up to 3 days.

When ready to serve, melt the combined oil and butter in a 12-inch skillet. Fry the sandwiches, 2 or 3 at a time, until they are golden brown.

Drain the sandwiches, cut in quarters, and serve them hot. Makes 24 hors d'oeuvres.

dill and sardine
sandwiches
norway

Open-faced sandwiches are popular on the smorgasbord table as well as at any light meal.

White or rye bread
Butter

Sardines, chopped
Dill pickle, chopped

Cut the bread into oblong shapes about 1 inch wide. Generously butter the bread strips.

Mix the sardines with enough dill pickle to suit your taste. Spread this mixture on top of the buttered bread.

If these sandwiches are to be used for a light lunch, you may prefer to quarter the bread instead of making oblongs. Either way, the taste is a treat. Make whatever quantity you need.

eggs stuffed with shrimp
denmark

1 4½-ounce can shrimps
6 to 8 hard-cooked eggs
2 tablespoons butter

Drain the shrimps, reserving the liquid.

Cut the cold, hard-cooked eggs in half lengthwise to make boats of the egg whites. Remove the yolks.

In a bowl mash the egg yolks fine with softened butter. Add enough of the reserved shrimp liquid to make a smooth paste.

Fill the egg halves with the paste so that the whites are covered. Top each egg half with as many shrimps as it will hold.

Chill the eggs and serve. Makes 12 to 16 egg halves.

jellied fish
sweden

2 or 3 pounds fresh fish
1 bay leaf
5 allspices
Salt and pepper to taste
1 tablespoon gelatin in ½ cup cold water

Cut up the fish and boil it with the spices in enough water to cover for ½ hour. Remove all bones and skin. Add the gelatin to the fish and water; pour the mixture into a greased mold.

Allow the jellied fish to set firmly before turning it out onto a platter. Garnish with parsley. Makes 8 or more servings.

anchovy sticks
sweden

10 slices bread, toasted and buttered
½ cup chopped green onions
½ cup chopped parsley
¼ pound butter
40 anchovy fillets

Cut each piece of buttered toast into 4 1-inch strips.

Mix together the chopped onions and parsley. Sprinkle the mixture over the toast strips. Top with 1 anchovy fillet on each toast stick, and dot with butter.

Bake the sticks at 375°F just long enough to heat through. (The best way to be sure this appetizer is just right is to try one—but you may want to eat the whole batch!)

Serve the sticks hot; allow 2 or 3 sticks per person. Makes 40 sticks.

horseradish ham rolls
denmark

This makes an excellent appetizer for the smorgasbord table but is also tasty when used as the focal point of a meal.

½ cup heavy cream
1 teaspoon sugar
2 tablespoons prepared horseradish
½ cup cooked macaroni
6 to 8 slices cooked ham
¼ cup shredded Swiss cheese

Whip the heavy cream and, when stiff, add the sugar and horseradish. Gently fold in the cooked macaroni. Spread this mixture on the ham slices and roll them.

When arranged on the serving plate, sprinkle the ham rolls with cheese. Makes 6 to 8 rolls.

sandwich island
iceland

4 tablespoons lemon juice
8 flounder fillets, fresh or
   frozen
6 tablespoons oil
1 teaspoon salt
3 tablespoons flour

sauce
1 medium cucumber
1 bunch dill
½ cup cream
1 teaspoon mustard
1 teaspoon lemon juice
Pinch of salt
Pinch of sugar

other ingredients
8 slices white bread
3 tablespoons butter
8 pieces green lettuce
½ bunch parsley

Add the lemon juice to the fish fillets and let them stand for 10 minutes.

Heat the oil in a pan. Salt the fillets and dip them in the flour. Fry the fillets to a golden brown on each side (about 2 minutes) and set them aside to drain on paper towels.

To make the sauce, peel the cucumber and dice it very fine. Chop the dill very fine. Beat the cream in a bowl until it is very stiff. Spice the cream with mustard, lemon juice, salt, and sugar. Add the cucumber and dill.

Remove the crusts from the bread and spread the bread with a thin layer of butter. Place the fish fillets on the bread and cover them thinly with sauce. Top each with another piece of bread, placing the buttered side to the bottom. Cut the bread in half.

Set the sandwich on a piece of lettuce and garnish it with parsley. Makes 8 servings.

pickled mackerel
sweden

3 red onions
1 cup plus 1½ tablespoons
   vinegar
Dash of salt
20 peppercorns

2 bay leaves
4 whole mackerels
1 bunch dill, chopped

Peel the onions and slice them into rings.

In a pot boil the vinegar, salt, peppercorns, and bay leaves. Set aside to cool.

Wash, clean, fillet, and halve the mackerels. Cut each piece in half again. Dry them thoroughly.

Put the fillets into a glass pot. Cover them with onion rings. Spread the marinade on top of that. Let stand for at least 24 hours.

Serve the mackerel with chopped dill. Makes 16 pieces.

swedish platter
sweden

When dining in Sweden, one finds eating is a culinary art as well as a taste treat. The food looks as good as it tastes.

The Swedish platter can be expanded to meet any number of guests and can use everything your kitchen and pocketbook allow. The main idea is to present the food in an attractive, appetizing manner.

Try marinated sardines with marinated onion rings, decorated with pickle slices. Many foods mix well with apple or cucumber slices. Serve halved kippers on top of scrambled eggs. Smoked fish goes well on thin slices of bread, topped with lemon juice. Try salmon rolls with horseradish-sauce stuffing, baked ham or bacon slices with grilled tomato on top, or stuffed eggs with caviar. The possibilities are endless. Lightly browned toast or the bread of your choice complements the platter as well as the palate.

herring rolls
sweden

8 herring fillets	Pinch of cayenne or sharp
½ cup milk	paprika
½ cup mineral water	Salt and pepper to taste
2 apples	½ teaspoon sugar
2 tablespoons lemon juice	8 teaspoons cranberry sauce
½ cup cream	1 red onion
1 small onion	½ bunch dill
½ cup sour cream	2 dill pickles

Place herring fillets in a bowl and sprinkle with milk and mineral water. Let them sit for at least 3 hours.

Core the apples and slice them in 8 pieces. Sprinkle them with half of the lemon juice.

Dry the fillets with a paper towel and roll them upright on the apple pieces. Place the rolls on a serving plate.

Beat the cream until stiff. Add the small onion, the rest of lemon juice, and the sour cream, sugar, and cayenne or paprika. Salt and pepper to taste. Spread the sauce over the herring rolls and crown each with a teaspoon of cranberry sauce.

Peel the red onion and cut it into rings.

Garnish the herring rolls with onion rings, dill, and sliced pickles. Makes 8 pieces.

smoked salmon and egg sandwiches
norway

White or rye bread
Butter
Smoked salmon, cut in thin
    slices
Hard-cooked eggs
Strips of boneless anchovy

Cut the bread for these open-faced sandwiches in either squares or rounds. Spread each slice generously with butter. Cover the bread with thin slices of smoked salmon. Sprinkle chopped, hard-cooked egg whites over the salmon and top that with hard-cooked egg yolks that have been put through a sieve. Add a strip of boneless anchovy on top, and serve. Make whatever quantity you need.

marinated salmon in dill
sweden

3 pounds center-cut fresh
  salmon, cleaned and scaled
1 large bunch fresh dill
¼ cup salt (coarse salt
  preferable)

¼ cup sugar
2 tablespoons crushed white
  pepper

Cut the fish in half lengthwise, and remove the backbone and small bones. Place half of the fish, skin-side-down, in a glass baking dish or casserole.

Wash and shake dry the dill and place it on top of the fish. Combine the rest of the ingredients in a bowl and sprinkle this mixture over the dill, covering the whole piece of salmon. Place the other half of the fish, skin-side-up, on the top.

Cover the fish with aluminum foil; on top of that place a platter holding 3 or 4 cans to make weight. Refrigerate the fish like this for 48 hours. Morning and evening during this period, turn the fish over and baste it with the liquid that accumulates. Separate the halves of fish and baste inside as well. Put the platter with weights back in the refrigerator each time.

When ready to serve, remove the fish from its marinade, scrape away the seasonings, and pat it dry with paper towels. Slice each half of the fish, skin-side-down, on the diagonal, removing the slice from the skin.

Serve the salmon as an appetizer or on sandwiches, with Mustard Sauce. Makes 8 to 10 servings.

mustard sauce
3 tablespoons sharp mustard
1 teaspoon powdered mustard
3 tablespoons sugar

1 tablespoon light wine
  vinegar
3 tablespoons brine

Mix the mustard, powdered mustard, sugar, and vinegar together in a pot. Add the brine slowly, and beat it well into a thick sauce. Pour it over the salmon when ready to serve.

marinated salmon in dill

soups

yogurt soup
norway

1 cup yogurt
½ cup sour cream
Salt
1 bunch dill or 1 tablespoon
  chopped dill

2 teaspoons brandy
½ pound crab meat
White pepper

Combine the yogurt, sour cream, and salt to taste; beat them until foamy.

Reserve several sticks of fresh dill for garnish; chop the rest. Add it to the liquid. Season with brandy and add the crab meat. Let the mixture sit in the refrigerator for at least 30 minutes, until chilled well. Season to taste and garnish with dill sticks.

Serve the soup cold. Makes 6 servings.

spinach soup
norway

2 pounds fresh spinach or 2
  packages frozen chopped
  spinach
2 quarts chicken stock
3 tablespoons butter
2 tablespoons flour

1 teaspoon salt
Dash of freshly ground pepper
⅛ teaspoon nutmeg
Hard-cooked egg for garnish
  (optional)

Thoroughly wash the spinach, then drain it. Chop it coarsely. If frozen spinach is used, thaw it completely and drain it.

Bring the soup stock to a boil in a 4-quart pot and add the spinach. Simmer it uncovered for about 8 minutes. Strain the spinach from the stock into separate bowls. Press the spinach with a spoon to remove most of the liquid. If desired, chop the cooked spinach even finer.

Melt the butter in the soup pot, then remove it from heat. Stir in the flour, being careful to avoid lumps. Add the liquid stock, 1 cup at a time, stirring constantly. Return it to the heat and bring it to a boil. Add the spinach, salt, pepper, and nutmeg. The soup will thicken slightly. Simmer it for about 5 minutes more.

Serve the soup, garnishing each serving with a few slices of hard-cooked egg, if desired. Makes 4 to 6 servings.

fish soup
denmark

1 pound fish fillets
2 tablespoons lemon juice
2 tablespoons aquavit
Chives
4 onions, peeled
1 leek
2 carrots
4 to 5 medium potatoes

3 slices bacon
4 cups beef broth or meat
  stock
Pinch of saffron
½ teaspoon basil
1 bay leaf
Salt and pepper to taste
Parsley for garnish

Drain the fish fillets and cut them into 1-inch pieces. Put them into a deep dish. Add the lemon juice and aquavit, and cover.

Finely chop the chives and peeled onions.

Cut the leek in half and then into pieces.

Peel and dice the carrots and potatoes.

Dice the bacon and put it into a pot, cooking it until it is just transparent. Add the onions and chives and cook for 3 minutes more. Let this mixture steam. Add the leek, carrots, and potatoes; steam for 1 minute more.

Pour in the meat stock and add the saffron, basil, and bay leaf. Cover and cook for 15 minutes. Then add the fish mixture with its liquid and simmer slowly for 5 minutes more. Season the soup with salt and pepper.

Serve the soup in bowls or in a tureen. Garnish with parsley. Makes 4 to 6 servings.

fish soup

beer and bread soup
denmark

1 small loaf dark rye bread
3 cups water
3 cups dark beer or ale
½ cup sugar

1 whole lemon (both juice and
    grated rind)
Light or whipped cream for
    garnish

Break the bread in small pieces into a mixing bowl.

Mix the water and beer and pour this over the bread. Allow it to stand for several hours.

When ready to serve, cook the mixture over a low flame, stirring occasionally, just long enough for it to thicken. (If the mixture is too thick, strain it through a coarse sieve.) Bring it to a boil and add the sugar, lemon juice, and lemon rind.

Serve the soup with a spoonful of light or whipped cream on top. Makes 6 to 8 servings.

leek soup
finland

3 whole potatoes
6 leeks
5 cups beef broth
Salt and white pepper to taste

2 egg yolks
6 tablespoons cream
Parsley for garnish

Peel and dice the potatoes.

Clean, wash, and cut the leeks into thick strips.

Simmer the meat stock, and add the diced potatoes to it, and cook it for 15 minutes. Add the leeks. Simmer 5 more minutes, taking care that the leeks remain firm. Salt and pepper to taste.

Remove 1 cup of the broth. To this add the egg yolks and cream. Slowly add this mixture to the soup. Heat, but do not cook any longer.

Serve the soup in soup bowls with parsley garnish. Makes 6 servings.

leek soup

14

orange soup
iceland

1 tablespoon cornstarch
4 cups water
1½ cups orange juice
¼ cup sugar
Whipped cream for garnish
Thin orange slice for garnish

Mix the cornstarch in ¼ cup of cold water.

Bring the rest of the water to a boil. Add the cornstarch mixture to the boiling water to thicken slightly. Add the orange juice and sugar.

Serve either hot or cold, garnished with a spoonful of whipped cream and a thin orange slice.

For a pudding, rather than a soup, add more cornstarch to thicken.

Makes 6 servings.

beef and cabbage soup
norway

½ pound diced beef
½ cup shredded cabbage
2 quarts beef bouillon or water
4 small potatoes, diced
1 carrot, diced
1 parsnip, diced
1 stalk celery, sliced
1 leek, sliced
Salt and pepper to taste

Add the beef and shredded cabbage to the liquid bouillon. Cook this for 1 hour.

Add all the vegetables to the soup and cook it until the vegetables are tender. Season with salt and pepper; serve. Makes 6 or more servings.

cold buttermilk soup
denmark

3 egg yolks
½ cup sugar
1 teaspoon lemon juice
½ teaspoon grated lemon rind
1 teaspoon vanilla
1 quart buttermilk

Beat the egg yolks lightly in a large bowl, gradually adding the sugar. Add the lemon juice, rind, and vanilla. Slowly add the buttermilk, continuing to beat (either with an electric beater on slow or with a wire whisk) until the soup is smooth.

Serve the soup in chilled soup bowls. Makes 6 to 8 servings.

carrot soup
finland

4 or 5 large fresh carrots or 2 cups canned carrots with stock
2 tablespoons butter
2 tablespoons flour
2 quarts milk
1 teaspoon salt
Sugar to taste
Parsley

Wash and scrape the carrots if you are using fresh ones. Cook them in lightly salted water until they are soft. Mash the carrots with their stock. (If using canned carrots, simply mash the carrots as they come from the can, reserving the stock for use in the soup.)

Melt the butter in a large saucepan. Add the flour, stirring with a wooden spoon until blended. Gradually add the milk (heat it first or let it come to room temperature). Allow this to simmer for 10 minutes, stirring occasionally. Add the carrots and the stock, salt, sugar to taste, and parsley.

Serve the soup piping hot. Makes 6 to 8 servings.

beet soup
finland

2 large raw beets
2 tablespoons butter
1 tablespoon flour
4 cups meat broth
2 teaspoons sugar

1 tablespoon vinegar
½ teaspoon salt
1 small raw beet
Sour cream for garnish
  (optional)

Wash the 2 large beets and cook them in salted water until tender. Drain, peel, and cube them.

In a 2-quart pot melt the butter, add the flour, and stir until very smooth. Add the hot meat broth. Stir the mixture until it comes to a boil. Add the sugar, cubed beets, vinegar, and salt. Cook the mixture over low heat for about 2 hours.

Grate the small beet. Sprinkle it into the soup before serving. Top with a spoonful of whipped sour cream if desired. Makes 6 servings.

cold potato soup
norway

4 potatoes
1 medium onion
2 cups milk
2 cups sweet cream
½ teaspoon salt

Dash of pepper, freshly
  ground
2 tablespoons butter
2 cups sour cream
1 teaspoon chopped chives

Cook the potatoes and onion together until well-done. Drain and mash them thoroughly.

Slowly bring the milk and sweet cream to the boiling point. Add the mashed potatoes, onion, salt, pepper, and butter. Allow them to simmer for no longer than 5 minutes. Chill them thoroughly.

When ready to serve, beat the mixture thoroughly with the sour cream.

Serve the soup in individual cups, sprinkling the top of each with some chives. Makes 8 servings.

hot potato soup
norway

3 tablespoons butter
3 leeks
4 large potatoes
¾ cup water

1 quart milk
Salt and pepper to taste
Paprika

Melt the butter in a 2-quart pot.

Wash and chop the leeks and sauté them in the butter.

Peel and slice the potatoes and add them to the leeks. Add the water; cover. Cook until both potatoes and leeks are soft enough to put through a sieve.

After the mixture has been put through the sieve, add hot milk to it, stirring constantly. Season with salt and pepper.

Serve the soup with a dash of paprika on top of each portion. Makes 6 servings.

cauliflower soup
norway

1 medium head cauliflower
1 teaspoon salt
6 cups water
2 tablespoons butter
2 tablespoons cornmeal

1 cube beef bouillon
1 egg, beaten well
1 cup cream
Parsley for garnish (optional)

Wash the cauliflower and break it into pieces. Cook it in salted water for about 10 to 15 minutes, until it is tender. Drain off the water into another pot.

Add the butter, cornmeal, and bouillon cube to the water. Boil this for 3 minutes. Add the egg and cream; stir. Last, put in the cauliflower pieces. Bring the soup to a boil but do not boil it.

Serve the soup with or without parsley garnish. Makes 6 or more servings.

fruit soup
norway

This soup may be served for dessert, as a first course, or even for breakfast.

½ pound pitted prunes	⅓ cup cooked rice
1½ cups currants	3 tablespoons tapioca
1½ cups raisins	½ cup sugar
2½ cups fresh apples	2 tablespoons lemon juice

Cover the fruit with cold water and bring it to a boil. Allow it to simmer until the fruit is soft but not mushy. Add the cooked rice to the fruit. Add the tapioca; cook until the mixture is clear. Add the sugar; cook for 2 minutes more. Set aside to cool.

When the mixture is thoroughly cooled, add the lemon juice. Makes 8 servings.

apple soup
denmark

1½ pounds tart apples	4 tablespoons cornstarch
2½ quarts water	Sugar to taste
½ lemon, sliced thin	¼ cup wine (optional)
1 piece of stick cinnamon	

Wash, quarter, and core the apples. Do not peel them. Cook the apples until soft in 1 quart of water with the lemon and cinnamon stick. Put the apples through a coarse sieve.

With the rest of the water, put the strained mixture into a pot and bring it to a boil.

Mix the cornstarch with ¼ cup of water and add it to the pot, stirring constantly. Add the sugar and wine.

Serve the soup hot. Makes 8 servings.

blueberry soup
norway

This soup is delicious served either hot or cold.

1 quart fresh blueberries, washed and drained	½ cup sugar
2¼ quarts cold water	Generous slice of lemon rind
	4 tablespoons cornstarch

Place the blueberries, 2 quarts of the cold water, the sugar, and the lemon rind in a 3-quart pot. Cook this over low heat only until the fruit is soft. Stir in the cornstarch mixed with the remaining ¼ cup of cold water. The mixture will thicken slightly. Makes 6 or more servings.

pea soup with ham
denmark

3 medium onions	1 pound ham
3 whole cloves	1 teaspoon marjoram
1 pound yellow peas	1 teaspoon thyme
4 cups water	Parsley for garnish

Dice 2 of the onions. Peel the third onion, but leave it whole. Stick cloves into the whole onion.

Put the diced onions, whole onion, peas, and water into a pot. Cook them for 20 minutes; add the ham. Add the marjoram and thyme and let it cook for at least 1½ hours. Remove the cloved onion and the ham. Cut the ham into thick slices. Season the soup with salt to taste.

When ready to serve, place a slice of ham on top of each serving of soup; garnish with parsley. Makes 4 to 6 servings.

vegetable soup
finland

1½ cups diced raw carrots
1 cup fresh green peas
1 cup cauliflower florets
½ cup diced new potatoes
½ cup fresh green beans, cut small
8 halves small red radishes
2 cups finely chopped fresh spinach

2 teaspoons salt
2 tablespoons butter
2 tablespoons flour
1 cup milk
1 egg yolk
¼ cup heavy cream
½ pound cooked, cleaned medium shrimps (optional)
Parsley or dill for garnish

Prepare the fresh vegetables as indicated in the list of ingredients.

Put all vegetables except the spinach in a 3-quart pot. Cover them with cold water and add the salt. Boil them uncovered for 5 minutes or until the vegetables are tender.

Add the spinach and cook for another 5 minutes. Remove the pan from the heat. Strain the liquid stock and put the stock and the vegetables into separate bowls.

Melt the butter in the soup pot over moderate heat. Remove it from the heat and stir in the flour. Slowly add the vegetable stock, then the milk. Beat well with a wire whisk.

Combine the egg yolk and cream in a small bowl. Gradually add 1 cup of the hot soup. Still using the whisk, add the mixture back into the soup. Bring it to a simmer. Add the vegetables and cooked shrimps; simmer uncovered for 3 to 5 minutes more. Add seasonings if necessary, such as more salt and pepper.

Pour the soup into a soup tureen or serve in individual bowls, garnishing each portion with the chopped parsley or dill. Makes 6 to 8 servings.

crab soup
denmark

1 bunch soup greens
2 tablespoons butter
1 onion, diced
½ pound perch fillets
1 quart water
½ pound frozen Greenland crab (thawed)

½ cup white wine
1 teaspoon salt
½ teaspoon white pepper
1 teaspoon curry
½ teaspoon herbs
1 bunch parsley

Clean, wash, and chop the greens very fine. Brown them lightly in hot butter with the diced onion.

Chop the fish fillets and add them and the water to the soup pot. Allow to simmer for 15 minutes.

Remove the fish pieces from the liquid mixture. Put the soup mixture through a sieve and pour the strained liquid with the fish back into the pot. Put in the fish pieces and add the crab meat. Pour in the white wine and add the salt, pepper, curry, and the herb mixture. Bring this to a boil but do not cook it.

Serve the soup at once with parsley sprinkled on top. Makes 4 to 6 servings.

eggs

baked eggs
sweden

In addition to being a delicious light supper dish, this is an easy treat for an informal brunch.

6 eggs	2 teaspoons sugar
1¼ cups milk	1½ tablespoons flour
1 teaspoon salt	½ cup cooked ham (optional)

Beat the eggs until light.

Measure the milk into a 2-cup measure. Add the salt, sugar, and flour to the milk. Mix this with the beaten eggs. Last, add the ham—finely diced. Pour the mixture into a buttered baking dish.

Bake the eggs at 425°F for 25 minutes or until the center is firm. Makes 4 servings.

omelet with anchovies
sweden

3 tablespoons anchovy paste or 6 to 8 anchovy fillets	6 eggs
	½ cup thin cream or milk

If anchovy fillets are used, line the bottom of a greased baking dish with the fillets. The egg mixture will be poured over them.

Separate the eggs, and beat the egg whites until stiff. Set them aside.

Mix the anchovy paste with the egg yolks. Add the cream. Fold the egg whites into this mixture.

Bake the mixture at 325°F for 20 minutes or until it is set in the center. Serve at once. Makes 4 or more servings.

egg cake with sausage
denmark

3 medium sliced boiled
  potatoes
1 8-ounce can cocktail
  sausages
2 tablespoons margarine

4 eggs, beaten well
¼ cup cream or water
Green peppers for garnish
1 or 2 tomatoes for garnish

Dice the potatoes and set them aside.

Slice the cocktail sausages into the same bowl.

Melt the margarine in a skillet and brown the potatoes and sausages together. Add the eggs mixed with the cream or water. Cook the mixture over slow heat until it sets firm in the center.

Turn the egg cake out on a hot platter and garnish with the green peppers and tomato wedges. Makes 6 servings.

scrambled eggs with chicken
sweden

8 eggs
1 cup cooked chicken
1 cup cream or milk
½ teaspoon salt

Dash of pepper
2 tablespoons butter
2 teaspoons chopped parsley
  or finely cut chives

Beat the eggs slightly. Add the chicken, cream, salt, and pepper.

Melt the butter in a frying pan and add the egg mixture. Stir lightly with a large spoon until the eggs are set.

Place the eggs on a serving plate and garnish with the parsley or chives. Serve at once. Makes 4 or more servings.

bacon and egg cake
denmark

½ pound bacon
6 eggs
1 tablespoon flour

½ teaspoon salt
½ cup milk
3 tablespoons finely cut chives

Cut each slice of bacon in half. Fry it lightly (do not let it become crisp) in a 12-inch skillet. Drain and set it aside. Remove all but about 1 tablespoon of bacon fat from the skillet.

Combine the eggs, flour, and salt in a bowl. Gradually add in the milk.

Over moderate heat, warm the fat in the skillet. Pour in the egg mixture and turn the heat down to low. Do not stir. Let the eggs set firm, about 20 minutes. When the mixture is firm, remove it from the heat.

Arrange the bacon slices and chives on top and serve directly from the pan. Makes 4 servings.

ham soufflé
denmark

2 cups cold cooked ham,
  minced fine
6 tablespoons butter or
  margarine
⅓ cup bread crumbs

¼ cup flour
1½ cups milk
3 eggs, separated
½ green pepper, minced fine
Salt to taste

Sauté the ham in 2 tablespoons of the butter or margarine until the butter or margarine is absorbed. Add the bread crumbs; blend well.

Melt the rest of the butter or margarine in another frying pan. Add the flour; stir until it is smooth. Add the milk slowly, stirring constantly. Add the beaten egg yolks to the white sauce. Next add the minced-ham mixture, green pepper, and salt to taste. Last, fold in the egg whites, stiffly beaten.

Pour the mixture into a well-greased baking dish. Bake it at 350°F for about 45 minutes or until it is firm. Makes 6 servings.

20

eggs
denmark

6 eggs
3 tablespoons canned
  condensed milk
1 teaspoon salt
Dash of pepper
1 teaspoon dried beans
2 pickles, sliced or diced
3 tablespoons chives
8 ounces Danish cheese, diced
3 tablespoons butter
2 tomatoes
2 tablespoons chopped dill

In a bowl mix the eggs with the condensed milk, salt, and pepper. Add the dried beans, pickles, 2 tablespoons of chives, and the cheese.

Heat the butter in a large frypan. Add the egg mixture; cover. Simmer it on low heat for 10 minutes.

While the eggs are cooking, wash, peel, and quarter the tomatoes.

When the egg mixture has set in the middle, place the tomatoes on top for decoration. Sprinkle with chopped dill and the remaining 1 tablespoon of chives. Makes 6 to 8 servings.

eggs

meat and poultry

swedish meatballs
sweden

1 medium onion, finely
  chopped
3 tablespoons butter
1 cup mashed potatoes
3 tablespoons bread crumbs
1 pound lean ground beef
⅓ cup heavy cream
1 teaspoon salt

1 egg
1 tablespoon chopped parsley
  (optional)
2 tablespoons vegetable oil

sauce
Fat from the skillet
1 tablespoon flour
¾ cup light or heavy cream

Cook the onion in 1 tablespoon of the butter until the onion is soft but not brown.

In a large bowl combine the onion, mashed potatoes, bread crumbs, meat, ⅓ cup heavy cream, salt, egg, and parsley. Mix them with a wooden spoon until well-blended. Shape the mixture into small balls about 1 inch in diameter. Put on a flat tray and chill for at least 1 hour before cooking.

Melt the remaining butter and the oil in a 12-inch skillet. Fry the meatballs on all sides until they are done through, about 8 to 10 minutes. Add more butter and oil if needed. Transfer the finished meatballs to casserole or baking dish and keep them warm.

To make the sauce, remove the fat from the skillet. Stir in the flour and cream. Stir constantly as the sauce comes to a boil and becomes thick and smooth. Pour it over the meatballs.

Serve the meatballs and sauce with broad noodles or potatoes.

Makes about 48 meatballs.

forcemeat
denmark

Forcemeat is really only meat, fish, or poultry ground several times. It is combined with eggs, milk, and bread crumbs or flour, seasoned to taste, and is used as meatballs, croquettes, or in any dish that calls for ground protein as its mainstay.

beef forcemeat
denmark

1 pound ground beef
¼ pound fat or suet
½ cup flour
2 teaspoons salt

½ teaspoon pepper
1 medium onion, grated
1 egg
2 cups milk

Grind the beef and fat together several times. Add the flour, salt, pepper, onion, and egg; mix them thoroughly. Add the milk gradually, being sure it is absorbed after each addition.

For a meat loaf, shape the forcemeat into a greased loaf pan. Bake it at 400°F for 1 hour. Makes 6 servings.

beef pie
denmark

2 layers pastry dough
1 large onion
1 can mushrooms
4 tablespoons butter

2 tablespoons flour
2 cups beef stock
Salt and pepper to taste
6 to 8 roast-beef slices

Line a deep pie pan or baking dish with pastry. Set it aside.

Peel and slice the onion. Drain the mushrooms, reserving the liquid. In butter, sauté the onions with the drained mushrooms; remove them from the butter. Add the flour to the butter; blend it until it is smooth. Gradually add the beef stock and the liquid from the mushrooms. Season with salt and pepper.

Put a slice of roast beef on the pastry dough in the baking dish. Pour a little sauce over this. Cover it with mushrooms and onions; continue layering in this way until all ingredients are used. Cover it with another layer of pastry dough. Pierce the top with a fork.

Bake it in a hot oven (400°F) for about 20 minutes or until the crust is evenly browned. Serve at once. Makes 6 servings.

beef roll
sweden

Leftover beef roll is just as tasty served cold the next day.

3 pounds top round steak, 1½
   inches thick
1 pound ground veal
1 cup chopped onions
½ cup bread crumbs

1 egg
1 cup chili sauce
Flour seasoned with salt and
   pepper

Pound the meat to ½ inch thick.

In a bowl mix the rest of the ingredients in the order given, except the seasoned flour.

Spread the veal filling over the round-steak slices and roll up the meat. Tie each roll with a string. Cover the outside of the rolls with seasoned flour.

Brown the rolls at 450°F for 10 to 15 minutes. Reduce the heat to 350°F and roast them for 1½ hours. Slice and serve the rolls. Makes 6 or more servings.

stew
norway

1½ cups raw beef, diced
½ pound fresh pork, diced
1½ cups cooked corned beef, diced
4 cups raw potatoes, cut in small pieces

1 onion, diced
About 2 cups beef stock
1 teaspoon salt
½ teaspoon freshly ground pepper

Slowly cook the raw beef and pork for ½ hour with enough stock to cover. Add the rest of the ingredients and let them simmer for at least another hour.

When the meat is tender, the stew is ready to serve. Makes 4 or more servings.

ham in madeira wine
denmark

1 smoked ham
4 bay leaves
8 peppercorns

8 whole cloves
1 bottle Madeira wine

Soak the ham in cold water overnight. In a large pot cover the drained ham with boiling water. Add the bay leaves, peppercorns, and cloves. Cook them slowly for 2½ hours. Drain off the liquid.

Pour the bottle of wine over the ham. Simmer it for at least ½ hour more, basting if necessary. Slice and serve it.

If a wine sauce is desired with the sliced ham, slightly thicken 2 cups of the wine liquid.

Makes 12 or more servings.

hot ham rolls with asparagus
denmark

18 asparagus spears (white or green)
6 slices cooked ham

1 cup medium white sauce
Parsley for garnish

Put 3 asparagus spears on each ham slice, and roll them up. Arrange the ham rolls in a greased baking dish. Pour your favorite white sauce over the rolls. Bake them in a slow oven (350°F) for 30 minutes.

Garnish the ham rolls with parsley, and serve. Makes 6 servings.

ham rolls with horseradish
denmark

½ cup heavy cream
1 teaspoon sugar
2 tablespoons horseradish

½ cup cooked macaroni
6 to 8 slices cooked ham

Whip the cream until thick. Add the sugar and horseradish, and fold in the macaroni. Spread some of the mixture on the ham slices and roll up the ham.

Garnish with shredded cheese or parsley. Makes 6 to 8 ham rolls.

chicken cutlets
sweden

2 tablespoons flour
2 cups chicken stock
3 egg yolks, beaten
3 cups diced cooked chicken
12 mushrooms, finely diced

Salt and pepper to taste
1 whole egg, beaten
Bread or cracker crumbs
Fat for deep-frying

Mix the flour with ¼ cup of the chicken stock. Add this to the rest of the heated stock. Stir until it is thickened. Add the egg yolks to the sauce. Add the chicken, mushrooms, and seasonings. Stir constantly as the mixture cooks for 5 minutes. Cool and then chill the mixture for several hours so it becomes stiff.

Shape the mixture into cutlets. Dip each cutlet into the beaten whole egg and then into the bread crumbs. Chill the battered mixture again.

Fry the cutlets in deep fat, and serve. Makes 6 servings.

meat loaf in sour-cream pastry
finland

sour-cream pastry dough

2¼ cups flour
1 teaspoon salt
12 tablespoons chilled butter

1 egg
½ cup sour cream

filling

4 tablespoons butter
¼ pound fresh mushrooms, chopped
3 pounds ground meat (beef, veal, or pork)
1 medium onion, chopped

¼ cup chopped parsley
1 cup grated cheddar or Swiss cheese
½ cup milk
1 egg plus 2 tablespoons milk for use on dough

Sift the flour and salt together into a large bowl. With two knives cut in the butter until the mixture is like coarse meal. In a separate bowl mix the egg and sour cream. Add this to the flour mixture until the dough forms a soft, pliable ball. Wrap the dough in wax paper and refrigerate for 1 hour. Next, divide the dough and roll out each half to a rectangle 6 by 14 inches. Save any scraps of dough. Butter the bottom of a flat cookie sheet or jelly-roll pan. Put one sheet of the pastry onto the pan.

Melt butter in a 12-inch skillet. Add the mushrooms and cook them for 6 to 8 minutes, until lightly colored. Add the meat and continue to cook until the meat loses all trace of pink color. Combine the mushrooms, cooked meat, onion, parsley, cheese, and milk in a large mixing bowl. Form the meat mixture into a ball and put it in the center of the dough. With your hands, very gently pat the meat into a loaf shape. Cover this with the second piece of pastry dough and seal the edges with a fork.

Moisten the dough with a pastry brush dipped in the egg and milk. Prick holes in the top of the loaf to allow steam to escape.

Roll out the scraps of dough and cut them into strips. Crisscross these over the top of the loaf to form a design. Again brush it with the egg—milk mixture.

Bake the loaf at 375°F for 45 minutes, when the pastry will be golden brown. Makes 6 to 8 servings.

chicken forcemeat
denmark

This can be used as dumplings in soup or as croquettes.

2½ pounds chicken, cooked
½ cup cold butter or margarine
2 tablespoons flour

2 eggs
2 teaspoons salt
Heavy dash of ground pepper
2 cups cream

Remove the chicken meat from the bones and grind it well with the cold butter 3 times. Add the other ingredients, mixing well after each addition. Add the cream last, gradually, being sure it is absorbed after each addition. Makes 6 servings.

curried chicken
denmark

2 small chickens about 3 pounds each
1 medium onion, chopped
⅓ cup margarine

1 light tablespoon curry powder
3 cups boiling water
2 teaspoons salt
¼ cup flour

Cut each chicken into pieces. Brown the onion in the margarine. Remove the onion and brown the chicken parts in the same fat. Replace the onion and add the curry powder. Pour the 3 cups of boiling water over the chicken and add the salt. Simmer until the chicken is tender.

Mix the flour with a little water and add it to the chicken liquid. Stir until it is thick and smooth.

Serve the chicken piping hot. Makes 6 or more servings.

meatballs I
denmark

1 pound finely ground veal
½ pound finely ground pork
1 small onion, grated
4 tablespoons flour
1 teaspoon salt
⅛ teaspoon pepper
1 egg, beaten
1¼ cups milk
Butter for browning

Be sure the veal and pork are thoroughly ground. Mix well the meat, onion, flour, salt, and pepper. Add the egg and milk a little at a time. Mix thoroughly until all ingredients are absorbed into the meat.

Melt a little butter in a skillet. Drop the meat mixture by tablespoons into hot fat, forming meatballs. Cook for about 10 minutes, until browned on all sides. Makes 6 or more servings.

meatballs II
denmark

1 pound veal
1 pound pork
1 tablespoon salt
½ teaspoon white pepper
¼ cup flour
4 eggs
½ cup light cream
1 cup milk
1 medium onion, chopped
1 tablespoon butter

Grind the veal and pork together several times. Put them in a large bowl. With an electric beater at low speed, add the salt, pepper, and flour. Add the eggs 1 at a time, still at low speed. Add the cream and milk.

Brown the onion in butter for just 5 minutes. Add this mixture to the meat. The meat should be mixed enough to be handled easily.

Shape the meat into oval cakes and brown them on both sides. Cook them over slow heat for 15 minutes. Because pork is included, these meatballs must be thoroughly cooked. Makes 6 or more servings.

veal scallops in sour cream
norway

4 veal scallops, no more than
   ½ inch thick
3 tablespoons butter
3 tablespoons vegetable oil
¼ cup finely chopped onion
1 cup sour cream
½ cup shredded Norwegian
   goat cheese
Salt to taste
Fresh ground pepper to taste

Pound the scallops to ¼ inch thick. Set them aside.

Melt 1 tablespoon of the butter and 1 tablespoon of the oil in a 12-inch skillet. Add the onion and cook it for 3 to 5 minutes; do not brown it. Take the onion from the skillet and set it aside.

Add the remaining butter and oil and fry the veal over moderate heat until golden brown, about 5 minutes per side. Keep the scallops warm in a low oven while you prepare the sauce.

Pour off most of the fat left in the skillet. Add the onions and cook again for 2 to 5 minutes. On a low burner, slowly stir in the sour cream and cheese. Continue stirring until the sauce is smooth. Add seasonings to taste. Return the veal to the sauce. Baste the meat and let it simmer for 2 minutes. Serve immediately. Makes 4 servings.

dumpling steak

dumpling steak
denmark

2 pounds chopped beefsteak
3 large onions, chopped fine
5 tomatoes, skinned and
   chopped
1 teaspoon salt
¼ teaspoon black pepper

Paprika to taste
1 tablespoon butter
Tomato quarters for garnish
Parsley for garnish
Onion rings for garnish

Mix the meat with the onions and tomatoes. Add the salt, pepper, and paprika. Form the ground beef into a large round dumpling and set it in a well-greased casserole. Dot the top of the dumpling with specks of butter. Bake it at 400°F for 1 hour.

Decorate the finished dumpling with tomato quarters, parsley, and onion rings. Makes 6 to 8 servings.

Picture on next pages: the smorgasbord

liver pudding

liver pudding
finland

1 cup white rice	4 slices cooked, crumbled
3 tablespoons butter	bacon
1 medium onion, finely	½ cup raisins
chopped	3 tablespoons dark corn syrup
1½ pounds calf or beef liver	2 teaspoons salt
2 cups milk	¼ teaspoon ground pepper
2 eggs	¼ teaspoon ground marjoram

Cook the rice in 4 quarts of boiling salted water for 12 minutes. Drain and set it aside.

In a heavy skillet melt 2 tablespoons of the butter. Add the onion and cook only until transparent. Set aside in the skillet.

Put the raw liver through a grinder until it is finely ground.

Combine the rice, milk, and lightly beaten eggs in a large mixing bowl. Add the cooked onions, bacon, raisins, and corn syrup. Season this with salt, pepper, and marjoram. Last, stir in the ground liver.

Generously grease a 2-quart casserole with the remaining butter. Pour in the liver and rice mixture. Bake the pudding in a preheated oven at 350°F for 1½ hours or until a knife comes out clean from the center.

Serve the pudding hot with lingonberries or cranberry sauce. Makes 6 to 8 servings.

pan-fried lamb slices
iceland

1 leg of lamb	Butter or vegetable shortening
2 or 3 medium onions	Salt and pepper

Cut the lamb into ½-inch slices. Peel and slice the onions and brown them in butter. Drain the onions and keep them warm.

Fry the meat slices in the same shortening; season with salt and pepper.

To serve, arrange the meat on a platter. Cover the slices with the drained onions and serve them with mashed potatoes and a salad. Makes 10 servings.

dill meat
sweden

2 to 2½ pounds lamb meat
  (breast or shoulder)
6 cups water
1 teaspoon salt
½ bay leaf
3 peppercorns
1 bunch dill
½ bunch parsley
1 piece of lemon rind
1 onion
3 whole cloves
2 or 3 carrots, peeled

sauce
1 cup meat stock (from cooked
  meat)
3 tablespoons butter
3 tablespoons flour
2 teaspoons sugar
1 bunch dill
1 tablespoon lemon juice
1 egg yolk

Put the meat in a pot with the water, salt, bay leaf, peppercorns, dill, parsley, and lemon rind. Peel the onion and dot it with cloves. Add this to the mixture. Cook it for 2 hours or until the meat is tender.

Forty-five minutes before the end of the cooking, add the carrots. When the meat is tender, remove the meat and carrots from the broth. Cut the meat in strips and the carrots in 2-inch pieces. Serve the meat and carrots together, well-heated, with the accompanying sauce.

Put the meat stock through a sieve. Melt the butter in a small pan. Stir in the flour; mix well. Stirring constantly, cook for 7 minutes. Add the sugar, dill, and lemon juice to the sauce. Remove the pot from the stove. Stir in a beaten egg yolk.

Serve this sauce separately from the meat.

Makes 6 to 8 servings.

lamb with cabbage
norway

2 pounds lamb or mutton
1 tablespoon butter
1 tablespoon flour
¼ cup water
1 head cabbage
1 teaspoon salt
¼ teaspoon ground pepper

Cut the lamb or mutton into bite-size pieces. On the bottom of a 3-quart pot melt the butter. Mix the flour with the water and add this to the melted butter. Mix well to form a paste.

Wash and drain the cabbage and cut it into small pieces. Put a layer of cabbage on top of the paste in the pot. Next add a layer of the lamb. Season each layer with salt and pepper and continue layering the cabbage and meat, with the cabbage on top. Pour in just enough water to cover the meat and cabbage. Cook them over a slow fire until the meat is tender, at least 1 hour.

Do not stir this; serve it in the layers. Makes 6 servings.

pork chops
with apples
denmark

Salt
1 pound pork chops (cut from
 a roast)
Black pepper

2 tablespoons butter
2 onions
2 apples
Parsley

Salt the pork chops and spice them with pepper. Heat the butter in a deep skillet and brown the meat. Add enough water so that the meat does not stick to the skillet. Cook the meat over a low heat for at least 60 minutes.

Peel the onions and cut them into rings. Core and peel the apples and cut each into eighths. Add the onions and apples 10 minutes before the end of the cooking period. Cook the ingredients until all are golden brown.

Remove the meat and put it on a serving platter. Pour the stock, onions, and apples over the meat; garnish with parsley. Makes 4 servings.

ham and
vegetable stew
norway

4 or 5 raw carrots, cubed
4 white turnips, cubed
1 pound fresh peas
Salt
1 slice cooked ham or 2 cups
 diced leftover ham

1 tablespoon flour
1 tablespoon butter
Chopped parsley for garnish

Cook the carrots and turnips with the peas in salted water to cover. Add the diced ham to the vegetables and the water in which they have been cooked, reserving ¼ cup of the vegetable water.

Mix the flour and butter with the reserved vegetable water. Add this mixture to thicken the stew slightly.

Before serving, garnish with the chopped parsley. Makes 4 to 6 servings

stuffed pork
tenderloin
denmark

1 pork tenderloin
12 prunes, pitted
4 tablespoons butter
1 teaspoon salt

Dash of freshly ground black
 pepper
½ cup water

With a sharp knife cut a slit in the meat deep enough to insert the prunes. After inserting the prunes, close the opening with skewers or wrap it with twine.

Melt the butter in a skillet and brown the meat on all sides. Sprinkle it with salt and pepper. Add the water; cover and cook slowly for 2 hours or until the meat is tender. Add water if needed. Slice the meat and serve it.

Add flour to the juice in the pan and thicken it slightly if gravy is desired. Makes 6 servings.

meat patties
denmark

½ pound boneless veal
½ pound boneless pork
1 medium onion, grated
3 tablespoons flour
1½ cups club soda

1 egg, beaten
1 teaspoon salt
¼ teaspoon pepper
6 tablespoons butter or
 vegetable oil

Have the butcher grind the meats together twice. Mix the onion with the meat. Add the flour to the ground meat, and mix well—an electric mixer can be used. Gradually add the club soda, beating until the meat is light. Last, add the egg, salt, and pepper. Cover the bowl and refrigerate it for at least 1 hour, so that the meat can be easily handled.

Shape the meat into 4-inch rectangles 1 inch thick. Melt the butter in a large skillet and add the meat patties a few at a time. Cook each batch at least 6 to 8 minutes per side. Since there is pork in the mixture, the meat must be cooked all the way through. The finished patties will be brown on the outside with no tinge of pink in the center. Makes 8 to 10 patties.

seafood

flounder with shrimp
denmark

Salt
4 fillets of flounder
Flour
2 eggs
2 tablespoons water
Dried bread crumbs
8 tablespoons butter
½ pound small cooked
   shrimps
Lemon wedges

Salt the fillets lightly and dip them in flour, being sure to shake off the excess. Beat the eggs together with the water. Put the bread crumbs on wax paper. Batter the fish by dipping each fillet first in the egg mixture and then in bread crumbs, coating each side thoroughly. Set aside the battered fish for at least 10 minutes.

Heat about 4 tablespoons of butter in a skillet. Sauté the fillets for 3 to 4 minutes. Keep them warm while you prepare the shrimps and sauce.

Melt 2 tablespoons of butter in a separate pan. Toss the shrimps in the butter so that each shrimp becomes coated with butter. Place shrimps down the center of each fillet.

Brown the remaining butter, pour it over the fillets, and serve. Makes 4 servings.

herring balls
sweden

1 medium salt herring or 4 herring fillets
1 small onion
1 tablespoon butter
1 cup cooked meat
4 medium cold cooked potatoes
1 tablespoon cornstarch
⅛ teaspoon white pepper
¼ cup milk or cream
Bread crumbs
Shortening for frying

If salt herring is used, clean the fish and soak it in cold water overnight. Fillet the herring.

Brown the onion lightly in butter. Grind the herring, onion, meat, and potatoes and mix them together in a large bowl. Add the cornstarch and pepper, mixing again. Add the milk or cream gradually—just enough to be able to shape the mixture into small balls. Shape the balls and roll them in bread crumbs.

Heat the shortening in a large skillet and fry the herring balls until they are brown on both sides.

Serve the herring balls with currant jelly or a hot currant sauce. Makes 4 to 6 servings.

herring and potato casserole
sweden

3 large potatoes
1 large onion
2½ tablespoons butter
2 matjes herring fillets cut in ½-inch diagonal slices
Freshly ground black pepper
1 tablespoon bread crumbs
⅓ cup light or heavy cream

Peel and cut the potatoes into ⅛-inch slices. Put them in cold water to keep them from discoloring.

Peel and slice the onion. Cook the onion lightly in 2 tablespoons of butter until soft and transparent.

Butter a 2-quart baking dish. Drain the potatoes and dry off any excess moisture with a paper towel. Put a layer each of potatoes, herring, and onion in the baking dish. Continue with alternate layers, ending with potatoes on top, and seasoning each layer with pepper. Sprinkle the top layer with bread crumbs and dot it with butter.

Bring the cream to a boil on top of the stove. Then pour the hot cream over the casserole.

Bake the casserole at 400°F for 1 hour or until the potatoes are tender. Makes 4 servings.

oysters and macaroni
norway

½ pound uncooked macaroni
3 dozen oysters
½ teaspoon salt
Paprika
¼ pound butter
¼ pound grated cheese
½ cup bread crumbs

Cook the macaroni according to directions on the box. Drain it.

Grease a baking dish and put in a layer of macaroni. Next, add a layer of oysters, salt, and paprika, and dot with butter. Top this with grated cheese. Continue in this way, with the layers ending with oysters on top. Sprinkle the top with salt and paprika.

Melt the rest of the butter and add the bread crumbs to it; sprinkle this over the oysters.

Bake the oysters and macaroni at 400°F for 15 minutes. Makes 6 or more servings.

fishballs
finland

2 pounds cod fillets
4 teaspoons lemon juice
1 can sardines in oil
3 tablespoons butter
Dash of pepper
1 large onion, finely chopped
½ bunch parsley
½ bunch fresh dill
2 eggs, beaten

2 rolls, crumbed
4 teaspoons aquavit
Parsley for garnish
Lemon slices for garnish

batter
2 eggs, beaten
4 tablespoons bread crumbs
Oil for frying

Rinse the cod fillets under cold water and dry them on paper towels. Cover fillets with lemon juice and let them sit for 5 minutes. Next, put the cod and the sardines through a food chopper. Reserve the sardine oil for future use.

Cream the butter in a large bowl. Add the fish and pepper. Add the onion, parsley, and dill. Last, put in 2 beaten eggs, the sardine oil, rolls, and the aquavit. Mix well and season to taste.

With wet hands form the mixture into balls that are pressed somewhat flat. Dip the balls into the 2 beaten eggs, then dust them with bread crumbs. Heat a generous amount of oil in a frypan. Fry the fishballs for about 15 minutes or until they are golden brown.

Serve the fishballs garnished with parsley and slices of lemon. Makes 6 servings.

fishballs

fish cutlets
norway

1 pound fish fillets	Salt and pepper to taste
1 tablespoon lemon juice	1 onion, finely chopped
4 leeks or 2 onions	4 tablespoons butter
2 eggs	2 tablespoons oil

Rinse and dry the fish fillets. Coat them with lemon juice and let them sit for 10 minutes.

Clean, wash, and cut the 4 leeks or 2 onions into rings. Drain them well.

Put the fish fillets through a food chopper. Mix the finely ground fish with the eggs, salt, pepper, and 1 onion. Form the mixture into balls and press the balls flat. Fry the fish balls in butter until browned on all sides. Keep them warm.

Lightly brown the leeks in oil for 10 minutes and serve them around the fish. Makes 4 to 6 servings.

fish cutlets

herring salad
finland

1 young white cabbage head
6 cups water
6 to 8 strips bacon
4 matjes herring
2 tablespoons wine vinegar
1 teaspoon sugar
Freshly ground pepper

Clean and wash the cabbage. Drain and slice it fine. In a large pot bring the water to a boil and add the cabbage. Let the water come to a boil again, then remove and drain the cabbage and allow it to cool.

Brown the bacon lightly and break it into small pieces.

Skin and fillet the herring. Wash and rinse the fish well. Cut it into fine strips.

Mix the cabbage, bacon, and herring in a dish and season with vinegar, sugar, and pepper. Cover the dish for 30 minutes, then serve. Makes 6 servings.

fish dumplings with crab sauce
denmark

1 pound pike or perch	½ cup bread crumbs
1 onion	1 teaspoon salt
1 tablespoon butter	Dash of pepper
2 egg whites	1 tablespoon meat broth
⅛ teaspoon cream	

Fillet the fish.

Peel and dice the onion. Cook the onion in butter until transparent.

Put the fish through a food grinder. Add the onion, egg whites, cream, and bread crumbs. Put the mixture through the food grinder again. Add the salt and pepper and form the mixture into dumplings.

Place the fish dumplings in a greased casserole and add the hot meat broth. Cover the dish and bake it at 350°F for 20 minutes. Serve the dumplings warm with Crab Sauce. Makes 6 to 8 servings.

crab sauce

3 tablespoons butter	Salt and pepper to taste
3 tablespoons flour	¼ pound crab meat
Fish broth from dumplings	1 can green or white
1 egg yolk	asparagus tips
2 tablespoons cream	

Heat the butter and add the flour, stirring constantly. Add the fish broth from the already baked dumplings and let this simmer for a few minutes. Add the egg yolk, cream, and salt and pepper to taste. Last, put in the crab meat and asparagus tips. Pour the sauce over the fish dumplings and enjoy.

fish dumplings with crab sauce

baked halibut
iceland

1 slice halibut, about 2 inches
   thick
3 tablespoons butter
1 teaspoon salt
Dash of freshly ground pepper
1 cup canned tomatoes
½ teaspoon sugar
1 medium-size onion
½ cup heavy cream

Pat the halibut dry on paper towels. Remove the skin. Put the fish in a buttered baking dish and sprinkle it with salt and pepper. Brush the remaining butter over the fish. Add the tomatoes crushed with sugar. Cover with thinly sliced onion.

Bake the fish for 20 minutes at 400°F, then pour the cream over it and bake it for 10 minutes more. Makes 4 or more servings.

crusted herring
sweden

8 green herring
2 tablespoons lemon juice
1 teaspoon salt
3 tablespoons fine herbs
2 tablespoons bread crumbs
Parmesan cheese
4 tablespoons butter

Fillet the herring carefully; wash and let them dry. Cover them with lemon juice and set them aside for 10 minutes.

Put the herring in a greased baking dish and sprinkle them with salt and fine herbs. Spread the bread crumbs and Parmesan cheese over that. Melt the butter and pour it over the fish.

Bake the fish for 20 minutes at 425°F. Serve it hot. Makes 4 to 6 servings.

crusted herring

baked fish fillets
sweden

4 fresh or frozen fish fillets
3 tablespoons butter
3 egg yolks
1 teaspoon salt
½ teaspoon paprika
1 small onion (3 tablespoons
   when grated)

3 tablespoons chopped parsley
3 tablespoons chopped capers
   (optional)
3 tablespoons lemon juice

Place the fillets in a buttered baking dish. Dot them with butter and bake them at 400°F for 12 to 15 minutes.

While the fillets are baking, cream the butter and beat in the egg yolks until they are light and fluffy. Add the salt, paprika, grated onion, parsley, capers, and lemon juice. Put the well-mixed sauce in a double boiler to keep it from hardening.

When the fillets are cooked, spread the sauce over them and return them to the oven for 3 to 5 minutes. Serve at once. Makes 4 servings.

minced fish
denmark

1½ pounds fish (cod,
   haddock, or salmon)
2 tablespoons salt
¼ pound butter

2 tablespoons flour
¼ teaspoon pepper
Milk or cream

Remove all skin and bones from the fish. With a spoon or an electric blender mince the fish until it is a fine, smooth mixture. Add the salt, and mince a little longer.

In a separate bowl cream the butter and add the flour and pepper. Add the butter mixture to the fish. Add 1 teaspoon of milk and work the mixture again. Add milk by teaspoonfuls only until the mixture is soft, not mushy.

Put the minced fish into a greased baking dish. Set the baking dish in a pan of hot water and bake it at 350°F for about 1 hour. Makes 6 or more servings.

boiled codfish
denmark

1 whole, cleaned cod
Salt
Melted butter
Chopped raw onions

Chopped pickled beets
Chopped hard-cooked eggs
Chopped parsley

Rub the fish, inside and out, with salt and let it stand for an hour. Place the whole fish in cold water to cover and bring it to a boil. Cook the fish slowly uncovered until it is tender. Remove and drain the fish.

Put the fish on a serving platter and pour melted butter over it. The other chopped vegetables may be arranged around the platter as a garnish that will complement the flavor of the fish. Makes 4 servings.

haddock and dill
norway

1 package frozen haddock
½ bunch fresh dill
2 or 3 sliced tomatoes

¼ cup water
½ teaspoon salt
2 tablespoons butter

Put the frozen haddock into a pot. (Do not thaw it.) Cover the fish with the dill and the tomato slices. Add the water and salt, and dot with butter. Cover the pot tightly. Simmer the fish for about ½ hour.

Serve the fish with boiled potatoes. Makes 3 servings.

baked salmon
denmark

1 large can red or pink salmon
½ teaspoon salt
⅛ teaspoon pepper
½ cup bread crumbs
2 tablespoons butter
2 cups milk

Remove the bones and skin from the salmon.

Place one layer of the salmon in a well-greased baking dish. Sprinkle this with salt and pepper. Add a layer of bread crumbs and dot with butter. Repeat this until the fish is used up and has crumbs on top. Heat the milk and pour it into the baking dish at the sides without disturbing the crumbs on top.

Bake the salmon at 375°F for 40 minutes. Makes 6 servings.

jellied fish in tomato juice
sweden

1 pound fresh salmon or trout
1 teaspoon salt
6 allspices
2 bay leaves
1½ cups tomato juice
2 cups water
1 bouillon cube
1 package unflavored gelatin

Boil the fish, salt, and spices in 2 cups of water until well-done. Cool the fish and pick out the bones and skin. Flake the fish and place it in a greased fish mold.

Strain the broth and return it to the stove. Add the tomato juice and bouillon and bring the broth to a boil. Add the gelatin to the hot broth and pour it over the fish in the mold. Chill it until firm and set.

Unmold the jellied fish onto a platter and garnish with parsley. Makes 6 servings.

salmon soufflé
sweden

1 can salmon, red or pink
2 tablespoons butter
1 tablespoon flour
1 cup milk
½ teaspoon salt
Dash of freshly ground black pepper
1 teaspoon chopped chives (optional)
3 eggs, separated
2 teaspoons lemon juice

Remove the dark skin and all bones from the salmon. Mash it with a fork.

Melt the butter on top of the stove; add the flour, and blend. Gradually add the milk, stirring until the sauce is slightly thickened. Add the salmon to the white sauce, and add the salt, pepper, and chives. Remove it from the heat.

Beat the egg whites until stiff.

Add beaten egg yolks and lemon juice to the salmon mixture. Last, fold in the stiffly beaten egg whites.

Bake the mixture in a greased mold at 350°F for 45 minutes. The salmon is done when a knife comes out of the center clean. Makes 6 servings.

baked shrimp and crab
sweden

1 cup boiled, clean shrimps
1 cup crab meat
½ cup pimiento
½ green pepper
1 small onion
6 eggs, well-beaten
½ teaspoon salt
Heavy dash of freshly ground pepper
1 cup bread crumbs

Cut up the shrimps fine and break up the crab meat. Chop the pimiento, green pepper, and onion. Mix them together well. Add the eggs, salt, pepper, and bread crumbs.

Grease a loaf pan or mold. Shape the mixture to fit the loaf pan. Set the loaf pan in a pan of water. Bake it in the water at 350°F for 30 minutes.

This loaf can be served as is or with a seasoned white sauce poured over it. Garnish with chopped pimiento. Makes 6 servings.

vegetables

mashed potatoes with apples
denmark

2 medium apples
3 large potatoes
½ cup water
2 cups milk, heated
3 tablespoons butter
2 tablespoons sugar
Salt and pepper to taste

Peel, core, and slice the apples; peel the potatoes. Cook these together in ½ cup of water until they are soft. Mash them together thoroughly. Add the milk a little at a time; be sure it is absorbed before each addition. Last, whip in the butter, sugar, salt, and pepper. The mixture will be a little softer than mashed potatoes but just as fluffy. Makes 4 to 6 servings.

asparagus with creamed shrimp
denmark

4 tablespoons butter
4 tablespoons flour
2 cups liquid drained from
    shrimps and asparagus
½ teaspoon salt
⅛ teaspoon pepper
2 cans shrimps
1 can asparagus, green or
    white

Melt the butter; add the flour, and blend. Slowly add the liquid, stirring constantly until the mixture thickens. Add the seasonings to the liquid; last, add the shrimps, reserving a few for garnish.

Lay 3 or 4 stalks of heated asparagus on buttered toast. Pour the hot shrimp sauce over this. Garnish with 1 or 2 shrimps on top. Serve. Makes 6 servings.

carrot pudding
finland

½ cup pearl barley
2 cups water
2 cups boiling milk
1 pound carrots

1 egg, beaten
½ teaspoon salt
2 teaspoons sugar

Cook the barley in 2 cups of water. Gradually add the boiling milk and cook the barley for 1 hour.

Peel and grate the carrots. Add the carrots, egg, salt, and sugar to the barley.

Pour the mixture into a buttered baking dish. Cover it with bread crumbs and dot the top with butter.

Bake the pudding at 400°F for 1 hour. Makes 4 or more servings.

potato pancakes with chives
sweden

2 tablespoons chives
4 medium baking potatoes
2 teaspoons salt

Several twists of freshly
  ground black pepper
2 tablespoons butter
2 tablespoons vegetable oil

First chop the chives and set them aside.

Peel and grate the potatoes coarsely into a large mixing bowl. The potatoes will accumulate potato water. Do not drain it. Mix in the chopped chives, salt, and ground pepper. Work as quickly as you can, so that the potatoes do not turn brown.

Melt the butter and oil in a 12-inch skillet. Drop the potato mixture by spoonfuls (2 tablespoons per pancake) into hot fat. The 3-inch pancakes will take about 3 minutes a side to become crisp and golden.

Serve them piping hot. Makes 4 servings.

stuffed onions
norway

6 large onions
2 tablespoons butter
1 pound ground beef or veal

1 teaspoon salt
¼ teaspoon pepper
1 cup beef stock

Peel the onions and cut a ½-inch slice from the top of each. Put these aside to use for a topping. Hollow out the centers of the onions to form holes for the stuffing. Save the center of the onions, and chop them fine.

Melt the butter and brown the chopped onions. Add the ground meat, salt, and pepper. Mix them well.

When the meat is browned, stuff the centers of the onions with the meat mixture. Put the top slices of the onions back on and secure them in place with toothpicks.

Put the onions in a baking dish and pour the beef stock over them. Bake them at 375°F for 1 hour or until the onions are soft. Makes 6 servings.

cabbage with bacon and dill
norway

1 small head cabbage
6 slices bacon
1 small onion
½ teaspoon salt

¼ teaspoon pepper
1 teaspoon dillweed or 3 dill
  leaves chopped fine

Wash, core, and slice the cabbage. Set it aside to drain.

Fry the bacon slices crisp and set them aside.

Slice the onion fine and brown it in the bacon fat. Add the salt, pepper, and dill. Last, add the drained cabbage. Cover, and simmer over a low heat until the cabbage is tender, about 1 hour. Add water if needed during the cooking.

When the cabbage is tender, remove it from the pan to a serving dish. Garnish with the bacon slices. Makes 4 or more servings.

red cabbage I

sour cabbage
denmark

1 head cabbage
2 tablespoons butter
2 tablespoons flour
1 teaspoon salt
1 teaspoon caraway seeds
2 cups water
2 tablespoons vinegar
2 tablespoons sugar
¼ cup wine (optional)

Shred the cabbage into a large pot. Add all the ingredients as listed. Cook over very low heat for at least 2 hours. Add more water if needed.

Just before serving, add the wine and mix thoroughly. Makes 4 to 6 servings.

red cabbage I
denmark

1 large head red cabbage
2 tablespoons bacon fat or oil
½ cup red wine
3 tablespoons red currant jelly
1 teaspoon salt
Dash of white pepper
Pinch of powdered cloves
1 tablespoon sugar

Wash, shred, and drain the red cabbage.

Heat the bacon fat or oil in a large pot. Add the cabbage and heat it for 5 minutes. Then add the red wine, currant jelly, salt, pepper, cloves, and sugar. Mix very well and continue to stir for a few minutes until all flavors are absorbed. Cover and cook the cabbage over low heat for 25 minutes.

Serve the cabbage hot. Makes 6 to 8 servings.

red cabbage II
denmark

Danish red cabbage is improved if made ahead and reheated. Recipes similar to this are found in both Swedish and Norwegian cooking. This is truly a Scandinavian dish.

1 large head red cabbage
4 tablespoons butter
2 tablespoons sugar
¼ cup water
¼ cup wine vinegar
1 teaspoon salt
½ teaspoon pepper
3 apples

Wash the cabbage and drain it well, then shred it. Melt the butter in a large pot and add the shredded cabbage. Add sugar, and stir well. Cook gently for a few minutes. Add the water, vinegar, salt, and pepper; cover and cook the cabbage very slowly for 1½ hours.

Core and chop the apples. (Peel them if you prefer, but the apple skin adds flavor.) Add the apples to the cabbage; cover this and cook it for another ½ hour. Add more sugar and salt if needed, and serve. Makes 8 to 10 servings.

roast potatoes
sweden

6 baking potatoes small
  enough to fit in a deep
  spoon
3 tablespoons melted butter
1 teaspoon salt
2 tablespoons bread crumbs
2 tablespoons Parmesan
  cheese (optional)

Preheat the oven to 425°F.

Peel the potatoes and put them in cold water to prevent discoloring. Put 1 potato in the deep spoon and slice it down to the edge of the spoon, making the slices about ⅛ inch apart. The spoon will prevent you from cutting through the potato. Return the sliced potato to the cold water and slice the others in the same manner. Drain the potatoes and pat dry. Put the potatoes, cut-side-up, in a large buttered baking dish. Baste them with some of the melted butter. Sprinkle them with salt and cook them for 30 minutes in the preheated oven.

Now sprinkle the bread crumbs over each potato and baste them with the remaining melted butter. Continue to cook the potatoes for another 15 minutes or until they are golden brown and tender. Parmesan cheese may be added 5 minutes before the potatoes are done. Makes 6 portions.

roast potatoes

salads

cole slaw and ham with sour-cream dressing
denmark

½ cup thick sour cream
¼ teaspoon salt
2 teaspoons sugar
2 teaspoons lemon juice or vinegar

1 cup shredded cabbage
½ cup chopped celery
½ cup diced apple
8 slices boiled or baked ham

Whip together the sour cream, salt, sugar, and lemon juice. Mix the dressing with the cabbage, celery, and apple. (The apple may be peeled or not, depending on your preference. The peel adds color as well as flavor.) Spread this mixture on a ham slice, and roll it. Makes 8 servings.

fresh mushroom salad
finland

1 cup water
1 tablespoon lemon juice
½ pound fresh mushrooms
¼ cup heavy cream
1 tablespoon grated onion

1 teaspoon sugar
Salt
Pepper
Lettuce leaves

Bring the water and lemon juice to a boil.

Wash the mushrooms and slice them thin. Add the mushrooms to the water and simmer them for 3 minutes. Remove them from the heat and drain them.

In a slightly chilled bowl combine the cream, onion, sugar, salt, and pepper. Mix the dressing with a spoon. Add the drained mushrooms and coat them thoroughly with the dressing.

Serve the salad on lettuce leaves. Makes about 4 servings.

egg salad
denmark

1 package frozen peas
¼ pound crab meat

6 hard-cooked eggs
¼ pound smoked salmon

marinade

2 tablespoons mayonnaise
½ cup sour cream
1 teaspoon salt
Dash of pepper

1 teaspoon sugar
1 teaspoon lemon juice
½ bunch parsley

Cook the frozen peas according to package directions. Let them cool, then drain them. Drain the crab meat. Shell the eggs and cut them in small pieces. Cut the smoked salmon in strips. Mix all ingredients carefully.

Mix the mayonnaise and sour cream until lightly foamy. Add the rest of the seasonings and the chopped parsley. Pour the marinade over the salad, mixing gently. Refrigerate the salad for 10 to 15 minutes.

Garnish with tomatoes and parsley and serve. Makes 6 servings.

beef, nut, olive, and egg salad
sweden

2 cups cooked, diced beets
1 cup chopped nuts
¼ cup sliced stuffed olives
French dressing

Lettuce leaves
4 hard-cooked eggs
Whole stuffed olives for
 topping

Mix the beets, nuts, and olives together. Add the French dressing and toss until all ingredients are well-coated. Arrange this on lettuce leaves.

Separate the egg whites from the yolks. Chop the whites fine and use them as a garnish around the mound of vegetables and fruit.

Press the egg yolks through a fine sieve and sprinkle them on top of the vegetable mixture.

Top the salad with a whole stuffed olive. Makes 4 servings.

ham salad
sweden

1 cup macaroni
4 cups salted water
2 cups diced cooked ham
1 banana
2 tablespoons lemon juice
1 stalk celery
½ small honeydew melon
1 small bunch Concord grapes
1 cup small peas

marinade
½ cup sour cream
2 tablespoons mayonnaise
1 tablespoon lemon juice
Salt and pepper to taste
Pinch of sugar

Place the macaroni in boiling water for 12 to 15 minutes. Drain the macaroni, cool it with cold water, and let it stand to dry. Mix the cold macaroni and the diced ham in a large bowl.

Peel and slice the banana and let it stand with half of the lemon juice. Chop the celery and mix it with the rest of the lemon juice.

Remove the seeds from the melon and cut it into bite-size pieces. Seed and halve the grapes. Drain the liquid from the peas. Mix all the fruit and the peas with the banana and celery, then combine this with the macaroni and ham.

Mix the sour cream and mayonnaise well. Add the rest of the ingredients. Spread the marinade over the salad and cover it.

Refrigerate the salad for at least 60 minutes before serving. Makes 6 to 8 servings.

stuffed cucumbers
denmark

1 or 2 large salad cucumbers
5 tablespoons vinegar
4 tablespoons oil
½ teaspoon salt
Dash of pepper

filling
¼ pound smoked salmon
⅛ pound herring fillets
1 hard-cooked egg
2 teaspoons horseradish

Wash the cucumbers and cut each into about 8 round pieces. (Leave skins on to add color.)

Mix the vinegar, oil, salt, and pepper, and marinate the cucumber pieces for 15 minutes. Remove the cucumber. Drain and dry it.

Finely chop the smoked salmon and herring. Dice the shelled egg fine. Mix this with the marinade from the cucumbers. Add the horseradish.

Hollow out enough of the cucumber pieces to put the filling in.

Garnish with parsley and surround with tomato wedges. Makes 8 servings.

cabbage salad
norway

**2 cups cabbage, finely
   shredded
1 medium onion
½ cup chopped parsley
3 tablespoons sugar
1 teaspoon salt
3 tablespoons vinegar
2 tablespoons water**

Wash, shred, and drain the cabbage. Thinly slice the onion, and separate it into rings. In a salad bowl toss the cabbage, onion rings, and parsley to mix.

In a small bowl dissolve the sugar and salt in the vinegar and water. Stir well until all the sugar is dissolved. Chill it well.

Add the chilled liquid to the cabbage when ready to serve. Toss together gently so that all the cabbage absorbs the flavor of the dressing. Makes 4 servings.

salmon and cucumber salad
sweden

**2 cucumbers, washed
½ cup French dressing
1 can salmon
⅓ cup thick mayonnaise
1 tablespoon juice from
   salmon
Salt
Chopped parsley or chives for
   garnish**

Cut the cucumbers in half lengthwise. Scoop out the seeds and some of the flesh to form a shell. Discard the seeds, but chop the cucumber taken out into small pieces. Marinate them in some of the French dressing for ½ hour.

Drain the salmon, reserving the salmon juice. Remove the skin and bones and flake the salmon into small pieces. Pour the remaining French dressing over the salmon and let it marinate for ½ hour in the refrigerator.

Thin the mayonnaise slightly with salmon juice. Drain the marinated salmon and mix it with the mayonnaise.

Salt the cucumber shells lightly and sprinkle them with chopped chives or parsley. Fill them with the salmon salad. Spread the marinated cucumber over the top. Sprinkle this with chives and top with a line of thick mayonnaise. Makes 4 servings.

sardine and beet salad
norway

**8 sardines, chopped
2 large boiled beets, diced
1 medium onion, minced
4 tablespoons oil
4 tablespoons vinegar
1 teaspoon salt
Dash of cayenne pepper
Chopped parsley for garnish**

Put together the sardines, beets, and onion in a large bowl.

Mix the oil, vinegar, salt, and pepper together until well-blended. Pour this over the sardine mixture.

Garnish with parsley on top. Makes 6 servings.

salmon and macaroni salad
sweden

1 teaspoon cream
1 teaspoon vinegar
½ teaspoon sugar
1 cup mayonnaise
1 can salmon

2 cups cooked macaroni
1 cup cooked peas
1 cup diced celery
1 cup cooked diced carrots
Lettuce leaves

Add the cream, vinegar, and sugar to the mayonnaise, stirring until all are well-mixed.

Remove the bones and skin from the salmon and flake it into small pieces. Add the macaroni and vegetables. Last, pour the mayonnaise mixture over the vegetable, macaroni, and salmon mixture; toss until they are covered.

Serve the salad on crisp lettuce leaves. Makes 6 or more servings.

mixed-vegetable salad
sweden

2 cups finely shredded raw
  cabbage
2 cups finely shredded raw
  carrots
2 cups finely shredded raw
  beets

2 cups seeded, finely shredded
  raw cucumbers
1½ cups thinly sliced radishes
1½ cups tomatoes
1½ cups French dressing

Crisp the cabbage, carrots, beets, cucumbers, and radishes in bowls of salt water. Skin, seed, and shred the tomatoes.

Drain all vegetables and fruit when they are firm and crisp. Arrange them in a deep salad bowl in circular heaps so that the colors add to the eye-appeal of the salad.

Just before serving, pour the French dressing over all. Makes 8 or more servings.

cucumber salad
norway

3 tablespoons boiling water
½ cup vinegar
3 tablespoons sugar
½ teaspoon salt

½ teaspoon freshly ground
  pepper
3 cucumbers

Combine all ingredients except the cucumbers in a saucepan. Bring them to a boil.

Thinly slice, but do not peel, the cucumbers. Pour the liquid over the cucumbers. Allow them to cool.

Serve the salad garnished with parsley. Makes 6 to 8 servings.

christmas salad
iceland

½ medium head red cabbage
1 tablespoon red currant jelly
1 tablespoon preserves or jam

Juice of 1 lemon (2
  tablespoons)

Shred the cabbage and put it under a weight for several hours. (A plate with tin cans on top can be the weight.) Drain the cabbage and put it in a large bowl.

Add the jelly and preserves to the lemon juice, mixing well. Toss this mixture with the cabbage until it is well-mixed. It will be a color symphony on any table. Makes 4 to 6 servings.

breads

orange bread
sweden

3 cups flour
3 tablespoons baking powder
⅔ cup sugar
1 teaspoon salt
1¼ cups milk

2 tablespoons melted butter
1 egg
Peel of 1 orange, finely
   chopped

Measure the dry ingredients into a 4-cup measure. Sift them into a mixing bowl. Add the milk, butter, and beaten egg and mix with a wooden spoon. Last, add the chopped orange peel. Place the mixture in a greased loaf pan, 9×5×2 inches, and let it rise for about 15 minutes.

Bake the bread in a moderate 350°F oven for 50 minutes. Makes 1 loaf.

salt horns
iceland

2 cups flour
3 teaspoons baking powder
1 teaspoon salt

⅓ cup butter
½ cup milk
1 egg

Sift the flour with the baking powder and salt. Cut in the butter with 2 knives, then add the milk. Knead the dough thoroughly on a floured board. When completely blended, divide the dough in half. Roll out half of the dough into a round. Cut the round into 8 wedges. Starting at the round edge, roll each wedge to make a horn shape. Put the horns on a greased baking sheet. Repeat this with the second half of the dough. Brush each horn with slightly beaten egg.

Bake the horns at 425°F for 15 minutes or until golden brown. Makes 16 horns.

easy christmas bread
norway

5 tablespoons butter
3 eggs
1 cup sugar
1½ cups milk
1 cup raisins

½ cup chopped citron
5 cups flour
2 tablespoons baking powder
½ teaspoon salt
½ teaspoon ground cardamom

Melt the butter in a small pan; set it aside.

In a mixing bowl beat the eggs well with the sugar. Add the milk, melted butter, raisins, and citron.

Sift the dry ingredients together. Add them to the liquid mixture, stirring vigorously. Divide the dough and put it into 2 well-greased loaf pans.

Bake the bread at 350°F for 1 hour. Makes 2 loaves.

sweet or salty pretzels

sweet or salty pretzels
sweden

1 package dry yeast
½ cup lukewarm milk
4 or more cups of flour
1 teaspoon sugar
½ teaspoon salt

2 egg yolks
½ pound butter
2 tablespoons kosher salt or 4
    tablespoons fine sugar

Dissolve the yeast in the lukewarm milk. Put the flour in a large bowl, making a depression in the center. Add the dissolved yeast and milk, the sugar, and the salt. Add 1 egg yolk and mix well. Liberally dot the mixture with ¼ pound of the butter; knead it quickly and lightly. Roll out the dough on a floured board to a large square. Dot this with the other ¼ pound of butter. Cover the dough and set it in the refrigerator for 15 minutes.

Put the dough on the flour-covered work surface and roll it out again to a square. The butter should now be worked into the batter. Knead the dough 4 times and let it rest in the refrigerator. Repeat this process again. Then let the dough rest for 30 minutes at room temperature.

Roll out the dough for the final time to about 1 inch thick and 10 inches long, so that you can cut sticks about 1 inch wide. Cut and form these sticks into pretzel shapes. Put them onto a greased cookie sheet. Brush the pretzels with egg yolk. Then sprinkle them with coarse salt or sugar, according to your taste.

Bake the pretzels at 425°F for 20 minutes. Allow them to cool before serving. Makes 18 or 19 pretzels.

lucia bread

lucia bread
sweden

St. Lucia of Syrakus was a young Christian murdered in the Middle Ages. The young maiden is traditionally remembered in Sweden by the baking of this bread for her holiday on December 13th.

1 package dry yeast	**½ teaspoon salt**
½ cup lukewarm milk	**4 tablespoons butter**
¼ cup sugar	**Extra flour for kneading**
3 to 4 cups flour	**1 egg yolk for glazing**
1 egg	**Dried currants for garnishing**
½ teaspoon saffron	

Dissolve the yeast in 2 tablespoons of milk which has been heated to lukewarm. Mix this with the sugar, flour, egg, and 2 more tablespoons of milk to make a dough. Cover the dough and place it in a warm spot to rise for 15 minutes.

Put the saffron into a bowl with 4 tablespoons of milk. Add the salt. Melt but do not heat the butter. Pour this over the saffron mixture. Add this mixture to the risen dough and knead thoroughly until the dough does not stick to the bowl. Cover the dough and again place it in a warm spot to rest for 30 minutes. If necessary or desired, knead and let it rise again.

On a floured board roll out the dough to ½ inch thick. Shape it into rolls about 8 inches long. These can then be worked into shapes of spirals, pretzels, or crosses. Place them on a greased baking sheet. Glaze them with the beaten egg yolk and dot them with dried currants. Bake them at 425°F for about 15 minutes.

Serve the Lucia bread warm with plenty of butter and hot coffee. Makes about 24 pieces.

lefser
norway

3 or 4 potatoes
¾ cup cold water
1 teaspoon salt
3 cups rye flour
1 cup wheat flour
Extra flour for kneading

Peel, wash, and dry the potatoes. Grate them into a large bowl. Add the water, salt, and the flours, and mix well. Let the dough stand covered overnight.

The next day, on a flour-covered board, roll out the dough very thin. Cut it into circles about 6 inches round. Place the rounds at least 1 inch apart on a greased baking pan. (This amount of dough will cover 3 pans.)

Bake at 400°F for 6 minutes. Then turn the lefser and bake it for 6 more minutes.

Serve the lefser fresh with plenty of butter. Makes 12 pieces.

lefser

coffee bread
finland

¼ pound butter
1 package dry yeast
¼ cup warm water
¾ cup warm milk
½ cup sugar
½ teaspoon salt
3 eggs

1 teaspoon ground cardamom
4½ cups flour
Almonds (or other nuts),
**   coarsely chopped**
1 tablespoon coarsely crushed
**   sugar lumps**

Melt the butter and set it aside to cool.

In a large mixing bowl dissolve the yeast in warm water. Blend in the milk, sugar, salt, 2 eggs, cardamom, and 2 cups of the flour. Be sure the mixture is smooth. Add the butter and then 2¼ more cups of the flour. Beat until all flour is absorbed.

Use the last ¼ cup of flour on the pastry board. Put the dough in the center of the board and knead it for about 10 minutes or until the dough is smooth and elastic. Put the dough in a greased bowl, turning it once, then cover it. Allow it to rise for about 2 hours or until doubled in size.

Divide the dough into 6 portions. Roll each into a 12-inch strand between your hands. Place 3 strands on the center of a greased baking sheet. Braid from the center to each end and seal the edges. Repeat for the second loaf. Cover them lightly and set them aside to rise slightly — about 30 minutes.

Beat the remaining egg and brush the loaves with it. Sprinkle the loaves with almonds (or other nuts) and coarsely crushed sugar lumps.

Bake the loaves at 350°F for 25 minutes. Cool them on wire racks. Makes 2 loaves.

rye crackers
iceland

½ teaspoon salt
4 cups rye flour

1 cup butter
1 cup milk

Blend the salt with the flour. Cut in the butter with two knives, as for pastry. Add the milk and mix it in well. Knead it with your hands until it is well-blended. On a floured board roll out the dough very thin. Cut it into squares or rounds. Put the crackers on a greased baking sheet and prick the center of each with a fork.

Bake the crackers at 450°F until lightly browned, about 10 minutes. Makes 6-dozen crackers.

picnic bread
sweden

2 packages dry yeast
2 cups lukewarm milk
1 egg
½ pound butter
½ teaspoon salt
1 cup sugar
2 teaspoons cinnamon
6 to 8 cups flour

topping
1 egg
2 tablespoons water
½ teaspoon salt
2 tablespoons sugar
2 tablespoons chopped
   almonds

Mix the yeast with 2 tablespoons of the warm milk. Add the egg. Warm the rest of the milk with the butter, salt, sugar, and cinnamon and add this to the yeast mixture. Add the flour gradually. Knead the dough until it no longer sticks to your fingers. Put the well-kneaded dough into a greased bowl and cover it. Set it in a warm place until it has doubled in size, about 30 minutes.

Shape the dough into 2 8-inch-long loaves. Put the loaves on a greased baking sheet and make crossed slices on the tops of them.

Make the topping by mixing the egg, water, and salt. Spread this over the loaves of bread with a pastry brush. Sprinkle the bread with sugar and then with almonds.

Wait at least 20 minutes for the bread to rise again before placing it in the oven.

Bake the bread at 400°F for 20 minutes. Makes 2 loaves.

butter rolls
denmark

1 cup hot water
4 tablespoons butter
¼ cup sugar
1 teaspoon salt
1 package dry yeast

¼ cup lukewarm water
1 egg, well-beaten
4 cups flour
Melted butter

Pour the hot water over the butter, sugar, and salt. Let it stand until lukewarm.

Dissolve the yeast in the lukewarm water. Add the dissolved yeast and well-beaten egg to the butter mixture. Add the flour and beat thoroughly. Refrigerate the dough for several hours or overnight.

Roll out the chilled dough on a floured board to ⅛ inch thick. Brush the top with melted butter. Fold the dough in half and again brush the top with melted butter. Fold the dough in half again. It will now be ½ inch thick. Cut it with a small round cutter. Place the rolls in greased muffin pans; cover and let them rise for at least 1 hour.

Bake at 400°F for about 20 minutes. Makes 2-dozen rolls.

rye bread
norway

1 cup water
1½ cups milk
1 teaspoon sugar
2 packages dry yeast

2 teaspoons salt
6 cups rye flour plus 1 cup
    extra for kneading

Add the water to the milk and scald it. Allow the liquid to cool to lukewarm.

In a large bowl add the sugar to the yeast; add 3 tablespoons of the liquid mixture and 1 tablespoon of flour. Mix thoroughly and let it rest for 15 minutes.

After 15 minutes add the rest of the milk-water liquid. Next add the salt and flour and knead the mixture thoroughly. A little flour on your hands will make the kneading easier. When all the flour is worked in and the dough is smooth and elastic, set it aside to rise in a warm place. Allow at least 1 hour.

After the dough has risen, beat it down and knead it again. Divide it in half and shape it into loaves in a well-greased loaf pan. Set them aside to rise again for at least 1 hour.

Bake the loaves at 350°F for about 45 minutes. Makes 2 loaves.

saffron bread
norway

2 cups milk
2 packages dry yeast
About 7 cups flour
½ cup butter
½ cup sugar
½ teaspoon saffron
2 eggs

¼ cup almonds, blanched and
    ground or chopped
½ cup raisins
¼ cup candied lemon peel, cut
    fine
Extra sugar for decorating the
    top

Heat the milk to lukewarm. Dissolve the yeast in the milk. Add the flour and let the mixture rise until doubled in size.

In a small bowl cream the butter and sugar together. Add the saffron and 1 beaten egg, mixing well. Blend these ingredients into the milk dough. Add the almonds, reserving some for the top; add the raisins and candied peel. Knead again, adding more flour if required. Shape the dough into 3 loaves. Set them aside in a warm place to rise again.

Just before baking, brush each loaf with beaten egg; sprinkle with almonds and sugar.

Bake the bread at 375°F for 45 minutes. Makes 3 loaves.

oat cakes
denmark

¼ pound unsalted butter
¼ cup sugar

2 cups instant oatmeal
¼ cup white corn syrup

Melt the butter in a 12-inch skillet. Add the sugar and stir with a wooden spoon until they are mixed. Do not let the butter mixture burn. Add the oatmeal and stir occasionally while it is cooking, 5 to 10 minutes. Remove it from the heat and stir in the corn syrup.

Rinse the cups of a muffin tin with cold water. Shake out the excess. Pack the bottom and sides of the muffin cups with the mixture. Refrigerate them for at least 3 hours.

Loosen the cakes from the muffin tin by running a knife around the edges. Slide out the cakes and serve. Makes 12 cakes.

desserts

swedish pancakes
sweden

3 eggs
2 cups milk
1 cup flour

6 tablespoons butter
½ teaspoon salt

With a rotary beater or a whisk, beat the eggs together with ½ cup of milk. Add the flour and beat to a smooth consistency. Beat in the remaining milk. Add the butter, melted, and the salt. The batter will be thick but smooth.

Lightly grease a large iron skillet. (You will only have to grease it once.) Drop the batter 1 tablespoon at a time for each pancake. The pancakes will be about 3 inches round. Turn them after the edges have browned, and cook them for another minute or 2.

Serve the pancakes with fruit preserves. Makes 6 to 8 servings.

baked apple cake
sweden

2 cups cold water
¼ lemon plus 2 teaspoons
   lemon juice
4 large, tart cooking apples
½ cup sugar
¼ pound butter (1 stick)

⅔ cup sugar
3 eggs, separated
½ cup ground blanched
   almonds
Pinch of salt

In a 2-quart saucepan combine the cold water, the juice of ¼ of a lemon, and the ¼ lemon. Halve, peel, and core each apple, dropping each into the lemon water to prevent discoloration. Stir in ½ cup of sugar. Bring this to a boil. Simmer it uncovered for 8 minutes or until the apples are tender. Drain the apples.

Grease a deep pie plate or shallow baking dish. Arrange the apple halves cut-side-down. With an electric beater cream the stick of butter with the ⅔ cup of sugar. Add the egg yolks, 1 at a time, the almonds, and the 2 teaspoons of lemon juice.

Beat the egg whites with a pinch of salt until stiff. Gently fold them into the egg-yolk mixture, using a spatula. Pour this over the apples. Bake this at 350°F for 20 minutes or until the surface is golden brown.

Serve the cake at room temperature. Makes 6 servings.

strawberry snow
finland

2 cups fresh strawberries
Sugar to taste

4 egg whites
¾ cup whipping cream

Sprinkle the strawberries with sugar to taste and crush the berries. Reserve 6 whole berries for decoration. Beat the egg whites until stiff.

Beat the whipping cream until stiff. Gently mix together the berries, whipped cream, and stiff egg whites.

Spoon this into dessert bowls. Put 1 whole berry on top of each serving. Makes 6 servings.

fruit soup
sweden

¾ cup dried apricots
¾ cup dried prunes
6 cups cold water
1 cinnamon stick
2 lemon slices

3 tablespoons quick-cooking
   tapioca
1 cup sugar
1 tart cooking apple
2 tablespoons raisins
1 tablespoon currants

Soak the apricots and prunes for 30 minutes in cold water in a 3-quart saucepan. Add the cinnamon stick, lemon slices, tapioca, and sugar and bring them to a boil. Reduce the heat and cover the pan. Simmer the mixture for 10 minutes, stirring with a wooden spoon to prevent sticking to the pan.

Peel and core the apple and cut it into ½-inch slices. Add the raisins, currants, and apple slices to the saucepan. Simmer for 5 minutes more. Pour the mixture into a serving bowl to cool. Remove the cinnamon stick; cover and refrigerate the soup.

This may be served in soup bowls as a dessert. Makes 6 to 8 servings.

cinnamon coffee cake
denmark

⅓ cup butter
¾ cup sugar
2 eggs
1 cup flour
¼ cup cornstarch
2 teaspoons baking powder
½ teaspoon salt
½ teaspoon ground cardamom
½ cup milk

topping
⅓ cup sugar
½ teaspoon cinnamon
¼ cup slivered almonds or
   chopped nuts

Cream the butter and sugar. Add beaten eggs. Sift the dry ingredients together and add them alternately with the milk. Put this in a round, well-greased baking pan.

Mix the topping ingredients and sprinkle the cake with the mixture.

Bake the cake at 375°F for 30 minutes. Makes 6 or more servings.

apple turnovers
denmark

1½ cups butter (or margarine)
4 cups flour
½ teaspoon salt
2 packages dry yeast
1 egg
Applesauce for filling

Cut the butter into the flour and salt with 2 knives. The mixture will be slightly lumpy.

Mix the yeast in a beaten egg until all yeast is dissolved. Add this to the flour mixture. Knead thoroughly with your hands. Roll out the dough on a floured board. Cut it with a round cutter at least 3 inches in diameter. Put a teaspoonful of applesauce on half of each dough round. Fold over the other half and seal the edges with a fork.

Bake the turnovers on a greased baking sheet at 425°F for 15 to 20 minutes. They may be glazed with your favorite icing when cold. Makes 12 or more pastries.

apple pie
norway

1 egg
¾ cup sugar
1 teaspoon vanilla
¼ teaspoon salt

1 teaspoon baking powder
½ cup flour
½ cup chopped nuts
1 cup diced apples

With a wooden spoon mix the ingredients in the order given, folding in the nuts and apples last. Put the mixture in an 8-inch greased pie pan. Bake it at 350°F for 30 minutes.

Serve the pie warm or cold. Makes 6 or more servings.

danish pastry
denmark

2 packages dry yeast
¼ cup lukewarm water
1¾ cups heated milk, cooled to lukewarm
½ cup sugar
½ teaspoon salt

½ teaspoon ground cardamom
7 to 7½ cups flour
2 eggs
1 pound butter or margarine
Raspberry jam

In large bowl dissolve the yeast in lukewarm water. Blend in the milk. Add the sugar, salt, cardamom, and flour sifted together. Add beaten eggs. Add ¼ pound of the butter, either softened or melted. Mix thoroughly (fingers may be used in a kneading motion) and set aside in a covered bowl to rise for 30 minutes.

Roll out the dough on a board (flour is not necessary) into a large rectangle. Dot ⅔ of this dough with a whole stick of butter. Fold the unbuttered ⅓ of the dough over half of the buttered portion. Then fold the remaining ⅓ to make 3 thicknesses. Seal the edges; cover the dough with a sheet of wax paper and a cloth. Let it rise for 20 minutes.

Turn the dough halfway around and repeat the procedure, making sure there are again 3 layers and using another stick of butter. Let the dough rise again for 20 minutes.

Turn the dough a third time and roll it out again. This time use the last stick of butter. Seal the edges as before and let it rise for another 20 minutes.

Shape the dough as desired. Crescents, combs, or envelopes may be used, or you might try the following. Divide the dough in 2 parts. Set aside 1 part. Roll out half of the dough into a rectangle 8 × 12 inches. With a knife cut the dough in strips about ½ inch wide. Curl the dough around itself to form a round Danish. (The size you use depends on the size pastries you prefer.) Put the round circles on an ungreased baking sheet. Put ½ teaspoon of raspberry jam (or your own preference) in the center of each Danish. When the baking sheet is full, set it aside to rise for another 45 minutes.

Bake the pastry in a hot oven (450°F) for 15 to 20 minutes. Eat and enjoy. Makes 40 or more pastries.

dessert pancake
finland

2 cups milk
1 teaspoon salt
1½ cups flour

2 eggs
2 tablespoons sugar
2 tablespoons butter

Mix the milk, salt, and flour to a smooth batter. Set it aside for 1 hour.

Just before frying, beat the eggs and sugar together and add them to the batter.

Melt the butter in a frying pan, greasing the sides as well as the bottom of the pan. Pour the melted butter into the batter, and mix again.

Put all the batter into the frying pan. Bake it in the oven at 425°F for about 25 minutes or until golden brown on top.

Serve the pancake with raspberry jam. Makes 6 servings.

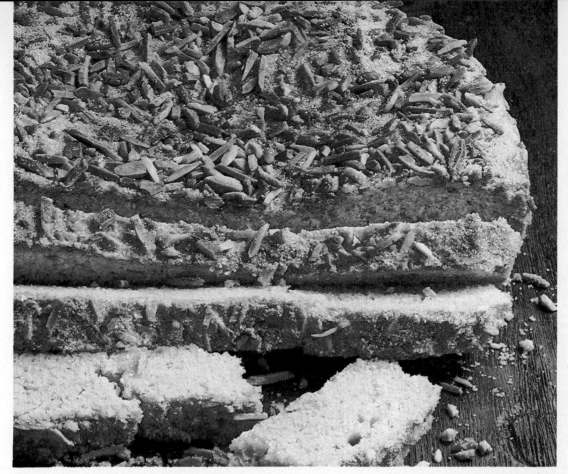

cardamom cake

cardamom
cake
sweden

4 cups flour
3 teaspoons baking powder
1 cup sugar
2 teaspoons cardamom
½ teaspoon salt

1 cup cream
¼ pound butter
Slivered almonds
1 teaspoon cinnamon
¼ cup sugar

Sift the flour and baking powder into a large bowl. Add the sugar, cardamom, and salt. Make a well in the center and pour in the cream. Mix together gently. Add melted and cooled butter and mix all together to a smooth dough.

Make the dough into a loaf shape about 10 inches long. Put it on a greased baking sheet. Sprinkle almond slivers over the top of the dough. Mix the cinnamon and sugar and sprinkle them over the top. Press the topping into the dough with your fingers. Bake it at 400°F for 45 minutes.

Allow the cake to cool and then slice it into thick pieces. Makes 12 or more slices.

coffee cakes
norway

¼ pound butter
¾ cup sugar
2 large eggs
½ cup cream

½ cup currants (or raisins)
1 teaspoon ground cardamom
2¼ cups flour
2 teaspoons baking powder

Cream the butter and sugar together. Add well-beaten eggs. Add the cream, currants, cardamom, and flour sifted with baking powder.
Grease small muffin tins and fill each cup ⅔ full.
Bake at 375°F for 20 minutes. Makes 3-dozen cakes.

59

applecake

applecake
iceland

¼ pound butter	1 cup sugar
2 cups bread crumbs	1 to 1½ cups applesauce

Melt the butter in a frying pan. Brown the bread crumbs lightly and stir in the sugar well.

In a deep glass dish or bowl place alternate layers of bread crumbs and applesauce, ending with bread crumbs on top. Chill it.

Top the cake with whipped cream if desired. Makes 6 servings.

applecake
sweden

¼ pound butter	2 teaspoons cinnamon
3 cups bread crumbs	2 cups applesauce
3 tablespoons sugar	2 tablespoons butter

Melt the butter in a pan. Add the bread crumbs, sugar, and cinnamon and stir until well-mixed and golden brown.

Place ⅓ of the bread-crumb mixture in a well-greased deep-dish pie pan. Cover this with 1 cup of the applesauce. Continue to layer with another ⅓ of the bread crumbs and another cup of applesauce. Put the rest of the bread crumbs on top and dot with butter. Bake it at 375°F for 25 minutes.

Serve the cake at room temperature. Makes 6 to 8 servings.

apple rings
denmark

3 or 4 large apples	¼ teaspoon ground cardamom
2 eggs, separated	2 tablespoons butter
2 teaspoons sugar	¾ cup milk
¼ teaspoon salt	1 cup flour

Peel, core, and slice the apples ½ inch thick.

Beat the egg whites until stiff and set them aside.

Beat the egg yolks and add the sugar, salt, and cardamom. Add melted butter, milk, and flour. Beat thoroughly. Fold in the stiffened egg whites.

Dip the apple slices into the batter and drop them at once into deep fat. Fry them until lightly browned. Drain the apples and sprinkle them with sugar.

Serve the apple rings warm. Makes 12 or more rings.

junk pastry

junk pastry
denmark

2 packages dry yeast
¼ cup sugar
1 cup milk
4 cups flour
2 egg yolks
½ teaspoon salt
4 tablespoons butter

Fruit marmalade or preserves
   for filling
2 extra egg yolks for garnish
Sugar for garnish
Chopped almonds for garnish

Dissolve the yeast and 1 tablespoon of the sugar in 2 tablespoons of warm milk. Let this sit for 10 minutes.

Sift the flour. Mix the yeast with the flour, the remainder of the sugar and milk, the egg yolks, and salt. Work this mixture until the dough is smooth and elastic and does not stick to your hands. Cover the well-worked dough and set it aside to rise for at least 15 minutes.

On a floured board roll out the dough to ½ inch thick. Dot it with 4 teaspoons of the butter and fold the dough together. Roll out the dough again, repeating this process until all the butter has been used. Let the dough rest for about 10 minutes.

Roll out the dough for the final time to ½ inch thick. Cut it into 4-inch squares. Place the marmalade or preserves in the center of each square and form the dough into horn- or pocket-shaped pieces. Place the pieces on a greased baking sheet. Coat the unbaked pastries with beaten egg yolks; sprinkle with sugar and almonds.

Bake them at 400°F for 20 minutes. Makes about 10 pastries.

61

fruit in cream
norway

2 apples
2 oranges
2 bananas

½ cup sugar
1 cup whipping cream
¼ cup chopped almonds

Peel all the fruits and cut them in slices or pieces. Sprinkle the sugar over the fruit. Let it stand for 10 minutes.

Whip the cream until stiff and fold it into the fruit.

Sprinkle the chopped nuts over the top and serve. Makes 6 servings.

egg dessert
norway

The Norwegian name for this is eggedosis, and it is often served in glasses for an eggnog type of drink as well as a dessert.

6 egg yolks
2 egg whites

6 tablespoons sugar
Brandy to taste

Beat the egg yolks and whites with an electric mixer until thick and lemon-colored. Add the sugar gradually, continuing to beat.

Use sherbet glasses, and place 1 teaspoon of brandy in each. Gently spoon the egg mixture over this. Makes 4 to 6 servings.

coffee fromage
norway

Fromage does not mean cheese in Scandinavia. It is a rich, molded dessert that can be made a day ahead of serving.

1 envelope gelatin
⅓ cup boiling water
2 cups heavy cream
⅓ cup sugar

⅔ cup cold strong coffee
Whipped cream for garnish
  (optional)

Dissolve the gelatin in boiling water and set it aside to cool.

Whip the cream until it is stiff, folding in the sugar and coffee. Add the cooled gelatin to the whipped-cream mixture and pour it into a mold or individual serving dishes. Chill it until set.

Garnish with whipped cream if desired. Makes 6 to 8 servings.

pineapple fromage
norway

1 envelope unflavored gelatin
⅓ cup boiling water
4 eggs, separated
1-pound can pineapple,
  crushed or chunks

½ cup sugar
2 cups heavy cream
½ cup pineapple juice
Whipped cream and pineapple
  for garnish

Soften the gelatin in the boiling water and set it aside to cool. Beat the egg whites stiff and set them aside. Drain the pineapple from the juice, reserving both.

Beat together the egg yolks and sugar at high speed on an electric beater. Add the cream, beaten until it is stiff. Add the juice of the pineapple, the cooled gelatin mixture, and the pineapple fruit. Gently fold in the beaten egg whites. Put the mixture in a mold and chill it for at least several hours.

When ready to serve, unmold the fromage on a serving plate and garnish it with whipped cream and pineapple. Makes 6 to 8 servings.

index